The Parker
Lifetime Treasury of
Wealth-Building Secrets

The Parker Lifetime Treasury of Wealth-Building Secrets

Edited and Compiled by

HERBERT F. HOLTJE

PARKER PUBLISHING COMPANY, Inc.

WEST NYACK, NEW YORK

Library of Congress Cataloging in Publication Data
Main entry under title:

The Parker lifetime treasury of wealth-building secrets.

    1. Success. 2. Finance, Personal. 3. Wealth.
I. Holtje, Herbert. II. Parker Publishing Company,
West Nyack, N. Y.
HF5386.P26   332'.024   77-11696
ISBN 0-13-650259-8

How This Book
Will Help You Become
Rich and Successful

There are many stories told in this book of people who have made great personal fortunes. But, the most important story of all is now being written; it's about you. It's about your life and what you will do with it. Yours is a story that you will write as you read the Wealth-Building Secrets that have turned ordinary people into millionaires. The story of your success begins now, as you follow the step-by-step directions in this book.

You can use the Wealth-Building Secrets in any endeavor you choose

Wealth can be made anywhere, in any field and by anyone. You may choose to build a business of your own, start a part-time venture or to advance to the top of the company that now employs you. Whatever your desire, you can make full use of every Wealth-Building Secret in this book.

Each Wealth-Building Secret has been carefully selected by

5

a panel of experts—people who have spent their lives in search of wealth. Their efforts have resulted in more than dreams for those who have followed them; they have lead to untold riches, personal success and even international fame. And, the people who have achieved these successes have not had the advantages of a special education or inherited wealth; they were people who knew that there was more to life than the 9 to 5 grind—and they wanted a life of comfort and pleasure, free from financial worry.

The first big step

Whenever you do something different, the first step is often the most difficult. The first time you take a boat out of the sight of land can be a frightening experience; but the next time, you never give it a thought. The same thing happens when you set out to build a fortune. All of the people whose stories are told in this book faced this same problem—and all of them solved it successfully.

Their accomplishments have been analyzed and described in this book so that your first step will be no more difficult than what you may be doing right now. To get you started immediately, the first chapter tells how to develop and use your own Million Dollar Mental Magnet. You will see how to expand your mind to visualize new wealth horizons so that you can instantly think, talk, look and act as though you already had the million dollars you will surely get. With this important concept firmly imprinted in your subconscious mind, you will then develop and use your own Money Blueprint for the Future.

A scientific program that insures success

You may want to think of each chapter as a personal lesson in prosperity, but don't think of this as a textbook. Rather, this is your personal collection of success-tested plans that you can use to build a fortune. And, each plan is explained in direct language so that you can put it into action immediately.

There are checklists, case histories, inventories, diagrams, and other dramatic illustrations to help you put the Wealth-Building Secrets into action. For example:

- You will use a scientific self-rating scale that will help you develop a powerful program of positive self-management.

- There are 13 outstanding techniques for personal development that have been part of the success of most of today's millionaires. They are revealed for you to use.

- It is possible to use Somebody Else's Money to build your own fortune. You can start a business immediately, without risking a penny of your own capital.

- You can get wealthy, famous and powerful people to help you put your Wealth-Building activities into high gear. You will learn how a simple formula—O.P.T.—can multiply what you already have and insure that profits will grow indefinitely.

- You must dominate people if you want to build wealth. When you use the special people-centered Wealth-Building Secrets, you will be able to influence and control just about anyone. You will be in command of yourself and others immediately.

- Could you use a million dollars worth of free advertising to get your Wealth-Building enterprise to the Blue-Chip stage? There is a chapter in this book that will make you an advertising expert, and give you the promotional leverage of a big company without costing a cent.

- Making money is one thing—making your money grow is another. You will learn how to build a Lifetime Treasury that delivers automatic dividends year after year.

- Start small—but never think small! Learn how to turn a second-income venture into a lifetime source of infinite riches!

- It takes money to make money: with the money you make using the Wealth-Building Secrets, you can make even more money. You will learn the secrets of successful investing. You can decide whether an investment will be good or bad for you, and then you can determine just how much money you can expect to make.

As you can see, this really is much more than a book. It is, indeed, a Lifetime Treasury of Wealth-Building Secrets. This is a program that meets the needs of everyone, at every step of the way. From Beginning Wealth-Builder to sophisticated investor, everyone will benefit from the information in this book. Even after you have gathered all the wealth you desire, this book will serve as a guide to personal wealth-management. After all, every millionaire must continue to prosper, to manage his money and to see that others have the same opportunity.

Will your story be told in a book like this next year? If you use the Wealth-Building Secrets that have made millions of dollars for those whose stories you are about to read, others will surely read of your success. Many fortunes are destined to be made—one of them can surely be yours.

                                            Herbert F. Holtje

ACKNOWLEDGMENT

Parker Publishing Company gratefully acknowledges permission to include in the *Parker Lifetime Treasury of Wealth-Building Secrets* chapters and adaptations from the following books:

Norvell, *Money Magnetism: How to Grow Rich Beyond Your Wildest Dreams* (West Nyack, N.Y., Parker Publishing Company, Inc. 1975)

J. V. Cerney, *Dynamic Laws of Thinking Rich* (West Nyack, N.Y., Parker Publishing Company, Inc., 1967)

Merle E. Dowd, *How to Earn a Fortune and Become Independent in Your Own Business* (West Nyack, N.Y., Parker Publishing Company, Inc., 1971)

Marian Behan Hammer, *The Complete Handbook of How to Start and Run a Money-Making Business in Your Home* (West Nyack, N.Y., Parker Publishing Company, Inc., 1975)

Herbert Holtje and John Stockwell, *How to Borrow Everything You Need to Build a Great Personal Fortune* (West Nyack, N.Y., Parker Publishing Company, Inc., 1974)

James K. Van Fleet, *Miracle People Power* (West Nyack, N.Y., Parker Publishing Company, Inc., 1975)

Duane G. Newcomb, *Spare-Time Fortune Guide* (West Nyack, N.Y., Parker Publishing Company, Inc., 1973)

Hal D. Steward, *Money Making Secrets of the Millionaires* (West Nyack, N.Y., Parker Publishing Company, Inc., 1972)

Scott Witt, *Second Income Money Makers* (West Nyack, N.Y., Parker Publishing Company, Inc., 1975)

CONTENTS

How This Book Will Help You Become Rich and Successful 5

1. How to Develop and Use Your Own Million Dollar Mental Magnet 17

Using the Wealth-Building Secrets to Build the Million Dollar Mental Magnet   18

The Millionaire's Secret Vow of Riches   18

Create your own Golden Hall of Fame . . . Take an inventory of your present treasures . . . Protect your image of wealth

Your Money Blueprint for the Future   23

2. How to Achieve Wealth-Mastery Through Positive Self-Management 29

"It's All in the Mind?"   30

Spark Your Career with the Personality Glow of Enthusiasm   31

Job-Enthusiasm Scale   31

Think Yourself Up the Glory Trail to Success   34

Emotion-Management Is a Necessity in Stepping Up to Success   35

How to Manage Your Future   36

13 Outstanding Techniques for Self-Management   37

The Art of Compromising and How to Do It   41

How to Retain the "Tough Line" in Self-Management   42

**3. How to Build Your Business Fast by Using Other People's
                              Money.** **47**

Your Wealth-Building Prospects with SEM (Somebody Else's
Money)   48

Getting the Money You Need to Start Your Business   50

> *Find how much money you need . . . Start-
> up expenses . . . Financial Plan (chart) . . .
> Operating expenses . . . Operating Plan
> (chart) . . .*

How to Scratch Up the Money You Need   60

> *Collect your sweat equity . . . Buy used tools
> and equipment . . . Tap new sources*

Money to Expand Your Business   63

> *Five-years Sales Projection (chart) . . . Capital
> Requirements Plan (chart)*

4. How You Can Tap the Money Sources of the Wealthy **69**

Exploring Your Sources of Capital   70

What You Should Know about Borrowing   73

Matching the Source of Your Capital with Your Need   75

Knowing about Bank Loans   77

> *Personal Financial Statement (illustration)*

Checking on Your Collateral   81

How Lenders' Limitations Can Affect Your Business   83

> *Loan Application (illustration)*

5. How to Get a Million Dollars Worth of Free Help from the Top People. 87

Getting Thousands of Dollars worth of Publicity—Free   88

Using O.P.T. to Build Success   89

Finding O.P.T. Everywhere   89

Getting Top Executives to Give You the Answers   90

How O.P.T. Can Multiply Your Resources and Profits   90

How to Make Other People Eager to Work for You   91

Tapping the Prime Source of O.P.T.   93

Discovering O.P.T. Within Walking Distance of Your Home 94

Using All Sources of O.P.T. to Build Wealth   95

How You Can Have a Million Dollar Sales Force for No Salary at All   96

How to Get a Network of Salesmen . . . Free   99

Solving All of Your Employment Problems . . . Without Charge   100

A Million Dollars Worth of Free Advertising Can Be Yours for the Asking   101

How Newspaper Editors Can Make You Rich   102

Tapping the O.P.T. of Educational Professionals   103

How to Make Other Professional People Anxious to Further Your Success   105

6. How to Control and Influence the People Who Can Help You to Succeed 107

How to Use a Person's Most Vulnerable Point to Your Own Advantage   108

Benefits You'll Gain   110

Techniques You Can Use to Gain the Benefits   111

*Knowing how you can fulfill a person's needs
. . . Finding out what a person wants . . .
Helping him get what he wants*

**7. How to Use Big-Time Advertising Secrets to Make Your
Business Grow** **119**

How to Make and Use News Releases Effectively   122

How to Make the Local Press Pay Off   123

How to Turn Television and Radio into a Gold Mine   125

How to Create a Splash—Locally and Nationally   127

Promote Yourself with the People Who Really Count   128

How to Use the Phone Effectively   129

How to Get Others to Sell for You   133

**8. How to Use the Selling Secrets of the Professionals to Build
a Fortune.** **133**

Changing to Sales   135

Sales Opportunities that Pay Off Big   140

Part-Time Selling—Key to Moonlighting Profits   143

Selling—the After-50 Opportunity   145

Your Step-by-Step Guide to Big-Profit Selling   145

**9. How to Build a Lifetime Treasury that Delivers Automatic
Dividends Year After Year** **149**

Some of the Ways   154

Two Essential Things   155

Five Steps to Take to Start on the Path to Riches   159

10. How to Turn Your Second Income Venture into a Lifetime
　　　　　　　　　　　　　　Fortune. **161**

　　Utilize Tax Advantages　　162

　　Put Your Surplus Cash to Work　　163

　　Combine Pleasure with Business　　165

　　Constantly Seek to Upgrade Your Second Job　　167

　　　　　　　　Increase your value to your employer . . .
　　　　　　　　Move to a bigger company . . . Train for a
　　　　　　　　better position

　　Guide the Expansion of Your Business　　170

　　　　　　　　Know when to make the change . . . Move
　　　　　　　　ahead with gusto

　　Enjoy the Fruits of Your Labor　　173

　　Learn to Apportion Your New-Found Wealth　　174

　　Your Kit of Wealth-Building Secrets　　175

11. How to Use Your Lifetime Treasury of Wealth-Building
　　　　　　　　　　Secrets Every Day of the Year **177**

　　How to Look for the Right Kind of Investments　　178

　　Where to Find Small Cash Investments　　179

　　　　　　　　Recreation or spare-time rentals . . . Musical
　　　　　　　　instruments . . . Back someone in a spare-time
　　　　　　　　business . . . Vacant land investments . . .
　　　　　　　　Resell used items . . . Need-filling investments
　　　　　　　　. . . Equipment rental investments . . . Bulk
　　　　　　　　lot investments . . . Farm machinery
　　　　　　　　investments . . . Resort area re-rentals

　　Don't Overlook Conventional Investments　　186

　　　　　　　　Second mortgages . . . Land . . . Mutual funds
　　　　　　　　. . . Limited partnership syndicates . . .
　　　　　　　　Apartments and duplexes . . . Stocks

How to Make Investments Fit Your Money-Making Plans
189

How to Test Your Investment Possibilities   193

> *Checklist for Successful Land Investment . . .
> Stability Table . . . Investment Success Table*

How to Get the Most out of Every Investment   202

> *Keep your dollars working . . . Keep good
> investment records . . . Shift money from
> unprofitable areas . . . Review investments
> regularly . . . Solicit referrals . . . Sell when
> you can make a good profit . . . Have an
> investment plan*

How to Pyramid Every Investment   206

> *Put profits back in . . . Sell and buy regularly
> . . . Use leverage whenever possible . . . Try
> to make one investment lead to others*

Investment Factors to Keep in Mind   208

The Parker
Lifetime Treasury of
Wealth-Building Secrets

1

How to Develop and Use Your Own Million Dollar Mental Magnet

You can magnetize your higher mind centers with a million dollar consciousness and begin instantly to think, feel, look and live like a millionaire.

It is in the mental realm that you first must begin to think you are going to be a millionaire. In the realm of the mind all things are possible. Mental concepts have always preceded physical action and material achievement.

It was in his mind that man first visualized himself flying like a bird. Realization of this dream came after he had built the consciousness that he could fly.

In back of every great fortune there is a million dollar mental magnet first. Every person who became a millionaire first had to think in terms of big money and success. A limited consciousness brings a limited income. When you expand your

---

From Norvell, *Money Magnetism: How to Grow Rich Beyond Your Wildest Dreams* (West Nyack, N.Y., Parker Publishing Company, Inc., 1975)

mind and visualize new money horizons, you will soon be using one of the most powerful Wealth-Building Secrets.

In this chapter we shall study the techniques for building the million dollar mental magnet, so that you can begin instantly to think, talk, look and act like you already have the million dollar fortune you are projecting.

USING THE WEALTH-BUILDING SECRETS TO BUILD THE MILLION DOLLAR MENTAL MAGNET

1. To imprint the idea of infinite riches on your higher consciousness, take the Millionaire's Secret Vow of Riches.

Every person who achieves a big fortune has made a secret pact with his higher, subconscious mind. Sometimes it is no more than just a mental determination to be rich and successful. Sometimes it is more clearly and deliberately stated in written or spoken form and becomes a dynamic command to the subconscious mind to build a fortune.

THE MILLIONAIRE'S SECRET VOW OF RICHES

Repeat the following Secret Vow of Wealth-Building every day for the next month, until it becomes so firmly engraved on your subconscious mind that it is an automatic part of your mental and physical reflex action.

I now take the Millionaire's Vow for Wealth-Building.
I recognize that there are infinite treasures in the Cosmic Cornucopia of Riches and Abundance. I draw upon the unlimited resources of the universe for my own enrichment.
I desire unlimited supplies of money and material

goods so that I may use my riches to help my family and to give something of value to the world.

I take an oath that I shall use money to help uplift those who are downtrodden; to liberate those imprisoned by poverty; to idealize the standards of the world; to strive to help children, the sick, the poor, the imprisoned, the blind and crippled, so they may know greater joy.

I shall use my money and earthly treasures to educate, inspire and uplift humanity; to help bring peace to the world, to banish discrimination and racial prejudice; to bring about equality for all; and to use my supply and abundance for the good of humanity.

When you once involve the Wealth-Building Secrets in your subconscious mind they begin to evolve the methods for you to achieve the fortune you desire.

A man who married when he was 24 was so poor that he didn't have the money to buy an engagement ring. On the day of his wedding he gave his wife a check made out for a date 25 years from that day for $25,000. He told his wife to cash the check on that future date.

Both of them forgot this beautiful wedding gift from a loving but poor husband, but the man's subconscious mind did not forget this vow of riches that was prompted by his loving heart. Exactly 25 years later this man was a millionaire, and one day his wife ran across the check and on their twenty-fifth wedding anniversary she cashed it without question or doubt that it would be good!

Such is the power of your higher mind when you program it with the million dollar mental magnet; it will set about automatically to bring you everything you involve in your higher mind centers.

Another interesting example of how the subconscious mind never forgets a vow of riches when it is sincerely made is that of another man who married a girl, with no future prospects that he would ever be rich. However, he vowed to her on their wedding day that on their tenth wedding anniversary he would present her with a special gift—a $10,000 string of real pearls. This man became a big business success in that period of time and right on schedule, he gave his wife a beautiful pearl necklace worth $10,000!

2. Create your own Golden Hall of Fame, where you join the invisible brotherhood of rich, famous and influential people.

To do this you obtain a scrapbook, the type you put snapshots in. Then cut out of magazines and newspapers the pictures and names of people who are rich, famous, successful, or gifted in some special way.

This Golden Hall of Fame can include movie stars, TV personalities, political figures, millionaires in industry, inventors, composers, great lawyers, doctors, explorers, writers, artists, space astronauts, sports stars, scientists, educators, religious leaders—in fact, any person you admire or that you wish to emulate and pattern your success after.

A few of these famous people you might want to add to your Golden Hall of Fame might be Onassis, Rockefeller, Howard Hughes, J. Paul Getty, Bing Crosby, W. Clement Stone, Churchill, the late President Roosevelt, or any other person you admire. If you do not have a photograph from a magazine or newspaper, just write down the person's name on the page. Then put your photograph on the same page with these famous and successful people.

Each night, just before going to bed, look at yourself in the Golden Hall of Fame with these illustrious persons and give yourself the following subconscious programming for riches.

I now elevate myself to the Golden Hall of Fame with the immortals, the rich, the successful, and I program my subconscious mind to make me worthy of a place alongside these illustrious persons.

I ask for the talents and the riches and recognition
that these people have earned, and promise myself
that I shall strive to be worthy of the high goals and
the riches that I ask for. I have confidence in my ability to rise to high places, and I now accept the glory
and recognition that shall be mine.

3. **Take an inventory of your present treasures; realize that you
may already be enjoying some things that all millionaires do
not now have.**

You cannot always equate money with happiness. You
may have the health, happiness and peace of mind that are
often denied to those who have millions. It is always good to
take a mental inventory of your present riches and to realize
that you may already have treasures that money in itself cannot
buy.

In the past few years five multimillionaires committed suicide! They had everything money could buy but they were so
miserable they could not face life. You can have millions and
still be happy, but without millions, you should not be miserable. If you correctly inventory your present treasures you will
find you may have more than many millionaires.

The Million Dollar Inventory should include:

A. Peace of mind.
B. Good friends who like you for yourself, not your
money.
C. Good health, mentally and physically, without pain or
anxiety about the future.
D. Love, happiness, marriage, a family of your own. These
are treasures money cannot buy.
E. Creative work that you enjoy and which you do not do
just for money, but for satisfaction.
F. Peace of soul with faith in God and spiritual security,

which give you the treasures of spirit, are often denied to those who make money their God.

To show you how millions of dollars do not always buy happiness, here is the story of a man who came into a barber shop to have his hair cut. It was obvious he was a very rich man by the way everyone bustled to wait on him. The manicurist rushed to his side; the shoe-shine boy began to polish his shoes; the barber practically bowed as he began to give him a haircut and shave.

The man had a big diamond stickpin in his tie, which was in the shape of a horseshoe. He wore a huge diamond ring on his finger. His clothes were tailor-made and obviously expensive. He was, one could see at a glance, a big shot.

When this man left the barber shop he gave everyone a generous tip and the barber turned to another customer and said, "Do you know who that man was?"

"No, who was he?" asked the customer.

The barber replied, "He's one of the big racketeers in this city. He owns race horses, has beer trucks, numbers rackets, and everything you could name that is illegal. He's worth millions of dollars."

Then he went on to say that the man suffered from high blood pressure, had recently had two severe heart attacks, his wife had just run off with a younger man, and his six-year-old son had just been run over by a truck—yes, you guessed it, by a beer truck! The barber went on to say, "That man's money can buy him everything but love, peace of mind, health, happiness, and his son's life."

The customer added, "His money can buy him everything but Heaven!"

Yes, you can have a million dollars and still be happy. But if you make money your God, you will probably lose out on the true spiritual, mental and moral treasures of life

4. Protect your image of the wealth you will one day have by

now taking a mental inventory of the things you want money for in the future.

Your subconscious mind will be deeply impressed by such a survey of the riches you hope to have and the things you wish to do with your money. You can call this projection of future wealth.

YOUR MONEY BLUEPRINT FOR THE FUTURE

Under this heading, list the things you want money for, and the sums of money you feel you need for future security. Your list might look like the following, or you can make up one to suit your exact needs.

A. I would like work in which I shall be able to make $15,000 a year to meet my future needs.

B. I would like to be in my own business making $50,000 or more a year. (Here, try to be specific telling your subconscious mind if you want a restaurant, a beauty shop, a health food store, a machine shop, a garage, an interior decorating business, a photographic studio; or some kind of business where you give service to the public such as accounting, repairing machines, income tax returns, health services, or any other special type of service.)

C. I would like to buy a new car of the following make, model and color. (Here describe the type of car you desire and the approximate cost. Do not be ashamed to buy a second-hand car if your pocketbook is not overflowing with money at present, for this is a beginning, and later it can be turned in on a new car.)

There is a story told about a very wealthy man who could afford to buy a new car every year. But for 25 years, he has bought a second-hand Cadillac with about 50,000 miles on it. He was told by a good mechanic that a Cadillac is just about broken in at that time and is a much better buy than a new car. He keeps the car an average of five years and then turns it in for another one, thus keeping up on modern mechanical improvements.

D. I want to buy a home of my own, in which to bring up my family and give them comfort and security. I want the house to be located in the country. (Here it is important to state the location you want, the style of architecture, the number of rooms and other details about its furnishings.) It is also important to pick the class of house you want; if it is to be a small cottage, obviously your money requirements will be more reasonable than if it is to be a mansion. It is important that you let your subconscious mind know what you expect, for it must prepare itself to reveal the mental magnet methods by which you can make the larger sums to pay for the bigger house.

For example: In California, a man and his wife learned about using the mental magnet for subconscious money programming. They were married and had two children, but the man was working for a salary in a leather goods store, where he was a salesman and made good commissions. However, they could never look forward to big sums of money or a big house.

This man had been reared in Texas and his father had a leather goods shop, where he manufactured hand-made wallets, handbags for women, make-up kits, and even fancy cowboy boots for rodeo stars.

The man was skilled at making leather goods and wanted to start his own business. But, he didn't have enough money.

He had a leather sewing machine in his home and decided to take orders for wallets, boots and handbags which he could make in his spare time.

He had cards made up, telling of his speciality in hand-made leather goods, and displaying a pair of cowboy boots, in color, on the front of his card.

He later told the astounding story of how his subconscious mind shaped his entire money-making desires into a practical idea to instantly bring him a bigger income.

A friend of his, for whom he had made a pocketbook without charge, received one of his cards. He worked in movie studios as a carpenter, and it just happened that he had met one of the big cowboy stars at that one studio. This man was always buying new boots, holsters, saddles, and other leather goods for his work. One day he called up this leather-worker and ordered a half-dozen pair of boots, a new holster, and other equipment, including a suede jacket for his wife. The upshot of this was that the movie star was so impressed by this man's work that he offered to back him in his own shop, and told him he could pay the money back as he earned it! If he lost, he could take it off his taxes!

With this big loan, the man from Texas opened a small leather business, hired three assistants, and with his connection with studios already formed, soon had other cowboy stars, recording artists and the general public as customers.

Now, exactly three years later, this man has one of the most successful leather goods manufacturing businesses on the West Coast. He repaid the movie star's loan, put a big down payment on his dream home out in San Fernando Valley, and is on his way to making his first million dollars!

E. I want the sum of $100,000 for future overall security, so I may have the leisure to travel, to advance my cultural interests, and to give my children a higher education.

This general, overall statement can include specific things you want in your life that will require large sums of money. If you know these things and write them down on your Future Money Inventory, they will be caught up in the automatic processes of your subconscious mental magnet and be more likely to evolve. If you do not have any such specific goals or sums of money in mind, you will never receive subconscious guidance to the achievement of your higher money goals.

A woman in California used this method to program into her subconscious mind that she wanted the sum of $1,000 for a specific immediate need. She had two children, a boy of 17 and a girl of 19. She wanted them to have a trip to Hawaii during their summer vacation. She and her husband had been to Hawaii on their honeymoon and she wanted her children to share in that wonderful trip, so they would have beautiful memories for the future.

Within one month, her husband received a $2,000 bonus for a big deal he had put over for his firm, and the entire family went to Hawaii on their vacation. If this woman and her husband had not projected these extra sums of money, he might not have had the inspiration to put over the big deal! Very often it takes such an emotional motivating desire to prod the subconscious mind to make that extra effort which can bring additional sums of money for specific purposes.

F. Carry at all times in your pocketbook a check made out to yourself for $1,000,000. *Sign the check, God, the Universal Banker.* Look at the check at least three times a day and begin to imprint on your subconscious mind the following programming:

> I now possess a million dollars or more in cashable assets. The resources of the universe are mine, as well as anyone else's. The gold, silver, oil, iron, uranium and all the products of earth, including agricultural ones, are mine. I possess the free parks, the museums, art galleries, public libraries and theaters. I own the subway and bus and other transportation. I possess the millions of dollars worth of entertainment on radio and television which I may have every day of my life. I now claim my divine inheritance and realize that now, in this moment, I have more than a million dollars in assets, which I may use and enjoy freely.

G. Form a Treasure Chest in which you magnetize the elements you desire in jewels, stocks, deeds to property, or other riches you want your subconscious mind to program for your future.

For this purpose obtain a small box, such as a man uses as a cufflink box, or a lady uses for a jewel box. Label this box MY TREASURE CHEST. Then put in the following items (if you do not have the real article, an imitation will do): A small piece of gold or silver and a bag of colored glass to simulate a diamond, pearl, ruby, emerald or other precious stone. Write down on small sheets of paper, THE DEED TO MY DREAM HOME. On another sheet write 1,000 shares of General Motors, or some other stock that you will find listed in the financial pages of the newspapers. Then take 10 pieces of paper and cut them the size and shape of money, and put in the four corners of each piece the sum of $10,000. These 10 sheets now number up to $100,000. You can count these over each night before going to bed, visualizing them as being real money, and day-dreaming on how you will spend this money.

If you wish to build the million dollar consciousness you can use the Treasure Chest principle by cutting out 10 sheets of paper and numbering them in the four corners with the figure of $100,000. These 10 sheets now add up to $1,000,000.

To treat your subconscious mind to a perpetual money feast, make it a point to look at your treasures each day at least once, preferably just before going to bed at night. Your subconscious mind will be deeply impressed by these objects, and you will be magnetizing your brain centers to respond with money-making ideas that will soon start the flow of money, goods and precious gifts into your life.

A young lady who used this method to bring her money or its equivalents had always wanted a big diamond ring. She was engaged at the time she learned about this method of subconscious mind programming, but her fiance did not have the money to buy her a big engagement ring. She began her Treasure Chest and put into it the dream home for the future, and a piece of glass which she mentally labeled as a diamond.

Within one week, her future mother-in-law called her on the telephone and told her she wanted to see her. When the girl arrived at her home the woman took out a small jewel case and said, "I don't know why, but yesterday something made me go to my safety deposit box at the bank and take out this jewel which my husband gave me 30 years ago. When he died I put it in the vault and have never worn it since."

The woman opened the little jewel box and there was a magnificent big blue-white diamond ring! She said, "Here, I want you to have it."

Later, this same girl, after she had married, received as gifts from her mother-in-law a string of real pearls, a ruby ring, a diamond and sapphire pin, and other trinkets that were given to her as gifts! Her million dollar mental magnet somehow sent out the cosmic command to the only source from which she could receive these treasures she had mentally programmed!

H. Create your Scrapbook of Destiny to build a million dollar mental magnet. Take an ordinary scrapbook and paste into it all newspaper or magazine pictures of houses, cars, furs, furnishings, or other objects you want to attract.

Besides actual pictures of objects, you may also put into your scrapbook any articles dealing with the lives of wealthy persons, their methods for building their fortunes, and items from the financial pages of newspapers about the stock market or big business. Let these financial items magnetize your subconscious mind with the consciousness of big money and methods that wealthy and successful people have used to build their personal fortunes.

Whenever you want to build a stronger mental money magnet, glance through your Money Scrapbook and read the various stories of how millionaires have built their fortunes. Then let the information sink into your subconscious mind. Later you will be automatically guided to take steps that cause you to attract money or get big business ideas that can make you rich.

2

How to Achieve
Wealth-Mastery Through
Positive Self-Management

Enthusiasm is self-generated. It's the master touch, the stimulus, the catalyst that propels you into action and creates the magnetic pull of your personality. Enthusiasm is a dynamo of action pulsing with the kind of power you need in trading up to success and the influence of power and control. It is the fire-in-the-furnace for thinking rich.

How dynamic you become depends on the self-inspiring message you give yourself each day. It depends on how well you develop the *posture-of-success* and maintain management of yourself. It's part of the *self-sell*. Take the following "sell" now and release it into your system! Do it over and over until it is ritual. Polish it! Smooth it! Use it until you are the very essence of what you want to be. Keep using it *not as a prayer* but as a forceful incentive plan with success already built in.

Here's what you can say—

From J. V. Cerney, *Dynamic Laws of Thinking Rich* (West Nyack, N.Y., Parker Publishing Company, Inc., 1967)

I am (your name)! I am a V.I.P.! Enthusiasm is my line and every day in every way I will walk tall, act tall and think tall on the road to success. I will think small about nothing! I believe in myself! I believe I am an important person. I feel great! I look great! I radiate! I did a terrific selling job yesterday and today I'll do even better. I'm on my way up and there's no stopping me. I will hurt no one in my forward motion. I believe in me and I, (your name), am going after everything I've ever wanted. Everything I have ever wanted is going to be MINE! Now get up and go!

Rehearse such a message as this before going in to sell a big account or enter a race. Step up those internal dynamos for full operational power! Notice how the feeling of euphoria that it inspires supports your *posture-of-success*. Notice how it prepares you for action and in this action is self-management at its best!

Remember that you are big league material all the way! You're tops in your field! You *believe* in you! You *believe* in self-management to lift you up out of mediocrity. You *believe* you have what it takes for success and you're going to use it! You believe in God, in your nation, in your business, in your career, and in yourself, and no one will stop you from reaching the top!

Use this kind of enthusiasm!

Use enthusiasm for all its worth and you will have that place in the sun that you desire!

"IT'S ALL IN THE MIND?"
YOU BET, FELLA, ALL THE WAY

It's indeed all in the mind . . . YOUR mind . . . in the Big Build-up. It's the personal pitch, the ego-lifter, the giant-maker. It's the message of enthusiasm that comes through loud and clear, the big push that propels you to the top and this means one thing—it means that you can step up to success through self-management, that self-management begins and ends in the mind's controls and compromises over which you have complete control.

If you think self-management doesn't work take a look at history. Take a look at the world's most outstanding men such as Darwin, Lincoln, Ford, Kennedy, da Vinci, Lister, on and on and on, all true stories with self-management as the key to their fame.

Certainly these men had wonderful assets, but so do you! Certainly these men worked for success, but so can you. Certainly these men had enthusiasm, but this trait can be yours as well.

SPARK YOUR CAREER WITH THE PERSONALITY-GLOW OF ENTHUSIASM

Performance on your job, no matter what your job or position may be, is determined by the character of your enthusiasm. It is determined by how you take on responsibilities, how you handle your job, how you THINK on and about your job, how important you think your job is to your company and to yourself, how you respect your job and how you show courtesies to others and what efforts you expend in doing your work each day.

To identify the relative amount of personal enthusiasm you have for your current occupation, take a piece of notepaper and write down numbers from 1 to 32 to answer the following personal admissions questionnaire. The answers will bring to light some very pertinently personal facts about your self-management.

JOB-ENTHUSIASM SCALE

Have you thought, or made, any of the following statements?

PART ONE

1. I'm a cog in a machine. Nothing else.
2. Sure, I'm part of the human inventory here but no one really knows I exist.
3. What this organization needs is a 25-hour week.
4. There's no job security here.
5. Fringe benefits? Three weeks with pay is a benefit?
6. I'm not getting enough money on this job.
7. I do the work. My boss gets the glory.
8. The Union should move in here.
9. So this kid just out of college moves in and makes more money doing less than I make for doing more.
10. We need a retirement plan and a sick-leave benefit that REALLY works!
11. Overtime? Not me, buddy. Eight hours a day is enough for me on THIS job.
12. What these bosses around here don't know is pitiful.
13. I simply can't stand these people around here. They're crude.
14. If I don't like the job I'll just quit!
15. Courtesy and respect for my job? What courtesy and respect does the Company show ME?
16. Sure I've walked off with Company property. The Company's so rich they'll never notice it.
17. This place is lousy with spies. You can't trust your best friends.
18. Any time you want the inside dirt on this Company let me know.

PART TWO

19. See that door? My name's going to be up there some day.
20. Being with this Company is exciting! It's going places and so am I!
21. Sure, boss, I'll be glad to put in overtime.
22. Tell me what you want and I'll carry the ball from there.
23. I'm not asking for special privileges. Of course I'll accept them but I'm more interested in the job that has to be done.
24. There are challenges everywhere in this organization and I'm going to try conquering them one by one.
25. Maybe no one knows me here right now but wait! The whole Company will know me in the future!
26. I've got what it takes for this job.
27. I may not have an intelligence quotient of 130 but I DO have a high Incentive Qualification and that's IQ enough for me.
28. I don't care how menial the job is! I'll do my best while I'm getting it done.
29. I keep coming up with new ideas for the Company all the time.
30. Do I plan on finding success here? I wouldn't have it anywhere else!
31. If it's good for the Company it's good for me.
32. My job is important to the Company and it's important to me. I'm giving it everything I've got.

Note: How many of the first 18 statements did you check positively? If you checked more than five you need self-management. Your thinking needs housecleaning. Now think in terms of Part Two of this questionnaire. These are the statements common to successful men. They are the statements of men who have themselves under control.

THINK YOURSELF UP THE GLORY-TRAIL TO SUCCESS

Industrial psychologist Mason L. Melling subscribes to the premise that a person's attitude toward his work, his boss, those around him, and the enthusiasm he generates determines the environment he creates.

Melling believes that if a company executive is apprehensive, fearful, uncertain, and out of control of his subordinates, he will generate apprehension and fear in others. To circumvent this Melling advises that people be secure, sincere, confident, and competent in public and others will see them in this light. When asked how one goes about achieving this state of mind he said—

"*Think* positively! *Think* you are among the best. *Think* about the top of the heap where you will soon be. *Think* you have courage and you WILL have courage. *Think* you have creativeness and inventiveness and it will be there. *Think rich!*

"Never punish yourself or incriminate yourself as being inadequate," he hastens to add. "*Think* yourself into being top-drawer personnel and that's exactly what you will be. Tell yourself you are the best until your gyroscope of self-respect becomes stable. Just stop thinking small! Answer all challenges with everything you've got and then add that little bit extra that it takes to make a champion.

"Close your eyes and ears to everything negative and you will not be negative. Hear no evil. See no evil. Manage your thinking and your mind will provide no place for evil. Your subconscious will not be fed disaster bait. You will have yourself under self-management."

EMOTION-MANAGEMENT IS A NECESSITY
IN STEPPING UP TO SUCCESS

Self-management begins and ends in the mind. It begins with voluntary controls and compromises and, in stepping up to success, self-management sooner or later is concerned with emotions.

Good or bad emotions are a series of mental pictures and words that stimulate an individual to fame and fortune. They may also bring about mediocrity and defeat it left unmanaged. Which end of the spectrum you develop depends on personal controls.

Emotions play a key role in human physiology. They play a powerful role in psychology as well. They make the difference between happiness and disaster and whether you think big or small determines your degree of success in the world.

"Happiness," says Melling, "is that feeling of good fortune, pleasure or gladness. Happiness is contentment that comes with accomplishing something good. It leads to peace-of-mind. When you have this you are big! You are rich within yourself!"

Fears, on the other hand, are the turmoil in one's thinking. *Fear is essentially emotion-mismanagement.* Fears are substantially real entities multiplying themselves through imagination until they breed a mountain of defeat.

Fear is an enemy, a detractor, a drainer of strength. It is a frustrating emotional pressure that squeezes the mind viciously and multiplies human hurt. In a lifetime both happiness and fear must be contained through self-management, if you would step unhindered into the future.

Automobile designer Harry Cantrell was such a case. He couldn't control himself. There was no self-management and Scotch whisky put him on the rocks. He'd go for months without hitting the bottle and then he'd hit an engineering slump on the drawing board and seek the nearest bar to find an answer. For ten years Harry had young designers under him who covered for him during his periodic absences. Then word got around and Cantrell hit the skids. None of the major automotive companies wanted him and his fears drove him to a suicide attempt. He was hauled out of the Detroit River. He made another big try with booze and heavy tranquilizer consumption but this didn't help. Finally, though, Harry realized that he was determined to live and make the most of his talents. He cut off the Scotch. Since he was dead as a designer in the Detroit area, he headed for the West Coast and landed a job designing plush, custom-built, streamlined cars for people with plush pocketbooks. With malleable fiberglass he created dream cars of tomorrow. These cars went on exhibit everywhere. They were proclaimed as "the cars of the future"—and—"20 years before their time." Harry Cantrell found himself. He stepped into the future as a new man the moment he got himself under control. Self-management was his major necessity.

HERE'S HOW TO MANAGE YOUR FUTURE

Self-management begins with recognizing your problems for what they are and admitting them.

To the person who is afraid, fear is very real. To those who would reach for fame, fear can be a saboteur, an alien agent bent on destruction. It can be death to desires and to goals.

Fear dries the mouth. It weakens the knees. It drains vitality and leads to destructive illness. It twists mind and body so that decisions become harder and harder to make. It destroys confidence until mind and body are without character.

President Franklin Delano Roosevelt once said in a time of national stress—"We have nothing to fear but fear itself"—and fear is indeed man's worst enemy. As the end result of emotion-mismanagement fear has to be eradicated. *HOW is this done?* It is done by doing!

Recognize fear for what it is!

Identify it!

Smell it!

Taste it!

When you know what it is DO SOMETHING ABOUT IT!

What can be done? How can such an emotion as fear be managed? The answer lies in disciplined action. It lies in constructive response and doing. It lies in self-management.

In an interview, automobile designer Harry Cantrell listed 13 gems—13 valuable pointers to a controlled new life.

13 OUTSTANDING TECHNIQUES FOR SELF-MANAGEMENT

1. Act the role of success.

No matter how bad current matters become *put up a successful "front." Look* your best no matter how rich or how poor you may be. Look like a million! Squeeze your buttocks together! Pull your belly in. Lift your cheeks and chest. Make your eyes laugh as you look at the world and at your objectives and I'll guarantee you won't be feeling gloomy. You can't! You'll be in the *posture-of-success* and that's the only way to go. So LOOK successful! FEEL successful! ACT successful and step-by-step SUCCESSFUL is exactly what you will be.

2. Never portray the role of defeat.

At no time, in words or action, ever demonstrate defeat or failure. Give no one a chance to see you courting disaster emotionally. Come up smiling no matter how you hurt. Remember that fear is a personal matter and the defeat of fear is requisite No. 1, so get moving! Do something directly remedial and you will not only set your recuperative powers going, but you will camouflage the depth of your hurt.

3. Accept criticism without resentment.

There will always be someone around to criticize you so accept it as par for the course. Also recognize the basis for criticism and rectify conditions that exist. Criticism from your worst enemy is often the best advice you'll ever get because *good* friends seldom tell the truth . . . that's why they're your best friends!

4. Blot out embarrassment.

If you are at fault be the first to admit it. Announce you are wrong and move on. Don't pause. Don't worry about it. Don't give it the time of day, and this mental-control-attack on embarrassment will be so defined as to keep your cheeks from flushing. Embarrassment, and its control, therefore, can be a constructive stepping-stone to self-management.

5. Step up confidence in yourself.

When emotional lows hit you, work a little bit harder. Give it that little bit extra so vital to championship performance. Above all DON'T RUN AWAY from responsibility. Step right into the action and slug it out. DO it and feel that new and wonderful expression of competence and confidence within yourself. *Get that golden glow that comes with faith and belief in yourself.*

6. Stop worrying about matters over which you have no control.

Adopt a "Ho hum, so what!" attitude about matters beyond your control. You can't stop a tornado but you can wait until the storm subsides to pick up the pieces and rebuild. The new building you erect may be of such design and strength as to resist tornados in the future.

7. Be decisive.

Make decisions when decisions are necessary. Don't procrastinate. Don't hesitate. If your idea is good or valuable, to you or to others, plunge into it. Of course there will be detractors and detracting factors but why be a rabbit all the time? Why keep running away? Why spend a lifetime complaining about the opportunities you muffed? *When you make your decisions don't deviate!* Maintain your confidence. Walk away from detractors. Allow no time for weepers, the worriers, the jealous or the pessimistic. They can destroy you and your emotional equanimity. They can destroy your confidence and your competence, so at the risk of being called a snob, turn around and walk away.

8. Accept loss gracefully.

If you have ever succeeded at anything you can be a success in the future. You can be a success again and again. Every day has one or more defeats and there are times when you wish you hadn't gotten out of bed. No day is a 100% success! Defeats are losses and whether they are business, social or economic losses accept them at face value. Write them off as an investment. Tomorrow you'll be just that little bit better for having had the experience and you will be prepared to conquer the same problem in the future.

9. Stimulate your brain.

Keep mentally fit at all times. Take new courses of study at night school. Stimulate your thinking and your imagination. Widen your horizons with new things and new thinking. Step over that horizon through learning and "mental fitness" will be yours.

10. Keep physically fit.

Use exercise to maintain your health. Do it regularly but don't overdo it. The week-end athlete is a handicap to himself when he overdoes it so be conservative, but be consistent. Work for physical fitness and your physical fitness will work for your mental fitness as well. Participation in athletics conditions you against fear.

11. Walk right up to what you fear.

It's quite possible that most of your fears are baseless. That boss you fear at the factory or office may actually be the best friend you'll ever have if you just step right up to him sensibly and be nice. Remember he, like other people, is human. He has his own problems in emotion management. Most of his problems are much bigger then yours so *YOU be the one to make the first step!* If at first you don't succeed, try and try again. Be persistent until recognized and smile all the while that you are doing it.

12. ACT! Never pause in indecision!

The old story about "He who hesitates is lost" is more then a cliché. It is a dominating and controlling force acting on those who pause when a decision is vitally necessary. Decision demands recognition of the assets as well as the deficits of anything! It demands sweeping away fear and diving in. It demands action! Action! Don't wait! DO!

13. Camouflage your defects and move on.

If you have a short leg, a club foot or hunchback don't spend the rest of your life apologizing for it. Everyone has a real or fancied defect of one kind or another so stop feeling self-conscious and sorry for yourself. Camouflage your defects and move on. Tomorrow is waiting for you . . . defects and all.

THE ART OF COMPROMISING AND HOW TO DO IT

Everyone needs adjustment to his surroundings. Everyone needs to compensate for his weaknesses and/or his disabilities even while recognizing his inadequacies and admitting them.

COMPROMISING is a settlement of differences by the use of concessions. It is an adjustment, an arbitration and yielding with the mental promise to abide by your own decision.

COMPENSATION is a behavior which makes amends for some negative factor or weakness. Thus, the art of compromising and compensating becomes a human necessity to survive in today's world. It is an even greater necessity for anyone who would think big or think rich.

To avoid isolation and unhappiness which comes to those who think big negatively (example: Hitler, Mussolini, etc), it is necessary to realize that an individual's thinking must vary from day to day.

The average person adapts and accepts rules and regulations. *The individual who thinks big takes these rules and regulations, expands them, and reinterprets them to fit his new and enlarged concepts.* Even while playing by the rule book he finds outlets through new avenues of expression.

In *the art of compromise* is the need to neutralize emotions. There is no need to dodge responsibility but there is a need to have an outlet and this may come through physical exercise or other social activity. It may come in any of the following methods that are given here to serve your purpose—

HOW TO MAINTAIN THE "TOUGH-LINE" IN SELF-MANAGEMENT

1. Recognize your zones of sensitivity.

Everyone has one or more business or socially sensitive zones. These *zones* may not be weak spots in your character but they may be embarrassing to those who have them. In compensating for your shortcomings develop that "So what!" attitude. Some of the world's greatest men were deformed and they made it to the top. There's lots of room up there! There's even enough for *you* if you learn to conquer your personality conflicts first.

2. Be competitive!

Go after what you want! Be in there to win! Fight for what you want and hold it! Maintain that tough-line and keep adrenalin and thyroxin flowing to maintain your drive. Use big thinking effectively at all times.

3. Make every defeat a step up!

When getting to a goal is temporarily impossible try another route. Admit your problem and move on. The experience will give you a new approach next time around. The good thing about a defeat is that it pinpoints your weaknesses so don't panic when hit by a loss or recession. Take advantage of it. Look at it as an opportunity! See it as an investment in understanding yourself a little bit better.

4. Gear down your emotional response.

In tapering off your emotional response to emergency don't use emotions as a dodge to evade responsibility. At the same time don't fail to find a controlled outlet for your emotions. Whether this outlet is in exercise or social activity siphon off the pressure. Develop a method of self-expression and find peace-of-mind.

5. Make a direct frontal attack on weakness.

In rearranging your thinking about your personal weak links admit your faults to yourself. Face up to reality. Admit them for what they are and then compensate for them. Develop a new standard of personal approach to life and gain that confidence and faith in yourself that comes with competence.

6. Set up new goals where necessary.

Maintain an elastic adaptability at all times. When one particular goal becomes patently unobtainable don't hesitate. Don't be frustrated. Don't even bother to be aggravated. DROP IT! Set up more obtainable goals but DO NOT AVOID COMPETITION! Do not resort to unfair methods of dishonesty in achieving such goals because this kind of limited, or small, thinking leads ultimately to failure and defeat.

7. Accept the glory of accomplishment without fanfare.

Within everyone is a basic desire for power and dominance. At one time or another no one escapes this feeling but in thinking rich DO NOT THINK OF POWER! Do not think of triumphing over others. SHOW HUMILITY for your accomplishments. Accept acclaim without further publicizing your talents. Your success will publicize itself.

8. Avoid unfair practice to gain attention.

It is possible, in the act of compensation, that an individual is dodging responsibility, that he is seeking escape, and as a result resorts to unfair tactics to gain additional attention. Attention is certainly due you. Everyone wants adulation and love but you personally don't have to resort to methods that hurt someone to get it. Keep thinking big. Keep thinking rich, but make it a Fair Practice Act never to be unfair about anything.

9. Give your ego satisfaction.

It is necessary to feed your ego and maintain self-pride. The control on this is *DO NOT OVERLY-COMPENSATE the satisfaction of your ego.* If you want prestige and acclaim *earn it!* Controlling your wishing is necessary as you go after your objectives. To desire ego-satisfaction is normal and healthy so maintain interests that intrigue you.

10. Avoid compensation in reverse.

Instead of dwelling on positive personality aspects in thinking big, some individuals attempt to hide their flaws with a device or performance designed to camouflage a deficiency. In thinking big admit your weaknesses to yourself. Then forget them. There's no need to compromise something that is unobtainable. There's no need to compromise or compensate for something that is completely lost in the shadow of your better talents, so forget it. Compensating in reverse is of no value so why fight it? Put the same amount of energy more profitably into something big. Think rich. If you want success in life, it is necessary to have successful self-management and self-management is the necessity of choice as you step into the future.

Self-management begins and ends with thinking. It begins with voluntary controls and compromises and the stepping up to self-control often begins with the emotions that have to be managed. Emotions play a powerful role in human physiology and psychology and they make a difference between happiness and disaster, and whether you think big or think little determines how well you function. It also determines the relative degree of your success.

Be totally self-conscious and aware of yourself in thinking big and thinking rich. Develop self-management for better living. Develop the assets of this dynamic law and remember that your success has its beginning in the psychology of the "pitch" you give yourself and the degree to which you keep yourself under self-management each day.

3

How to Build Your Business
Fast by Using
Other People's Money

Money—yours or somebody else's—means survival and profits. Study after study points out these salient facts—

- Lack of money, undercapitalization, or whatever you call it leads to about one-third of the business failures recorded.
- Money available for operations and growth promotes profitability—"them that has do better than them who don't" or "the rich get richer."

Both of these points demand your attention. You can't escape the need for money to start, maintain, and expand your business.

From Merle E. Dowd, *How to Earn a Fortune and Become Independent in Your Own Business* (West Nyack, N.Y., Parker Publishing Company, Inc., 1971)

YOUR WEALTH-BUILDING PROSPECTS WITH
SEM (SOMEBODY ELSE'S MONEY)

"Borrowing money to make money" makes sound business sense. Here's why—borrowing money (by whatever method you choose, as defined later) enables you, as the profit-oriented owner of a business, to expand sales, introduce new products, and decrease costs. Any one or all of these effects in combination should increase earnings more than the cost of the borrowed funds. For example, suppose you borrow $10,000 at 8 percent interest. At the end of the year, you will pay the banker $800 for the use of the funds plus the $10,000 principal (just to keep the figures simple). However, the $10,000 for a year enables you to build parts worth $40,000 when sold at retail at a cost of $20,000. A factor of two to one is not uncommon in make-or-buy situations for a small company. So, by borrowing $10,000 you rent equipment and hire labor, and save $20,000 on the cost of parts you sell or install as part of your business. At the end of the year, you pay off the loan plus the interest and retain a profit of $9,200.

Take an even more common example. You are pressed for funds in operating a retail or service business. So, you use suppliers' credit as part of your capital. This simply means that you order things from a wholesaler on credit. You hope to turn over the goods and collect cash from your customers in time to pay the suppliers' bills by the 10th of the following month. Your suppliers' funds become part of your capital. Most suppliers recognize that extending credit increases their cost of doing business. Money is a capital resource just as much as a delivery truck. Everybody pays rent for using money; the rent is called interest. But, instead of raising their prices to everybody, suppliers frequently offer a discount for prompt payment. Invoices may read—"2 percent 10, net 30." Such notation offers you a discount of 2 percent of the total billing if you pay within ten days. But, if you don't have the cash, you wait the full 30 days and pay the full amount. You are, in effect, paying 2 percent for using the money (credit extended) 20 days. On an annual basis, 2 percent for 20 days amounts to 36 percent interest on equivalent capital. To take advantage of cash discounts, you need a revolving cash fund big enough to carry purchases with your own money. By borrowing an amount equal to your purchases for 20 days at 10 percent, you earn the difference—or 26 percent. You can look at this transaction either of two ways: first, by using Somebody Else's Money (SEM), your business earns a 26 percent return on purchases completely outside your buy-and-sell activities; second, by reducing your costs of capital, you can price your goods and services competitively with other properly financed businesses.

When Mike Kinder took over a failing drive-in and turned it into a $30,000 profit in one year, he invested practically no money of his own. Note these steps—

1. Mike agreed to take over all obligations of the owner-manager simply by agreeing to pay off the $45,000 bank loan outstanding. The owner gave up his equity to protect himself from further losses. The bank permitted Kinder to assume the loan because of his proven credit and known managerial ability.

2. Supplies for the first month were delivered—again on Kinder's credit.

3. Wages and promotional expense were his only out-of-pocket payments.

4. At the end of the year, the drive-in business had become so profitable that Kinder sold his equity (difference between outstanding debts and capitalized earning capacity) for $30,000. But instead of taking the appreciated value in cash, he accepted a note for regular payments and interest at 8 percent. Kinder invested no long-term capital of his own in the venture—only his established credit. The bank and certain suppliers provided the required capital—Somebody Else's Money (SEM).

GETTING THE MONEY YOU NEED
TO START YOUR BUSINESS

You will need money in your business at least twice: (1) when you start, and (2) when you need to expand your business. Requirements for getting money differ at these two stages. So consider getting money to start first. Later, consider raising money to expand and enlarge your business.

Find how much money you need

Too little capital may mean failure before you ever get started for any one of a variety of reasons. Statistics muddy the primary cause for failures, and many failures termed as "managerial incompetence" may really have been financial failures. Aside from the specter of outright failure, too little opening capital adds these problems to your others at start-up—

Limits your stock of goods for sale.

Reduces your ability to advertise and limits your other business-development activities.

Forces you to use credit at noncompetitive rates.

Penalizes pricing due to an excess of fixed costs (loan interest, lease payments, etc.) during start-up phase.

All of these problems point up the need for a firm plan— particularly a financial plan—before you start. Chart 3-A defines a bare minimum Financial Plan. Note that it consists of two parts, start-up expenses and operating expenses.

Start-up expenses

These will occur only once. Later you may incur one-time expansion expenses. But, consider each of the one-time costs for starting your business—

CASH REQUIREMENTS	RENT	BUY
Start-Up Expenses:		
1. Facilities Down Payment		
2. Equipment		
3. Inventory		
4. Legal		
5. Advertising & Promotion		
6. Miscellaneous—		
a. Licenses		
b. Telephone Installation		
Sub-Total		
Operating Expenses—Per Month		
1. Rent		
2. Equipment rentals		
3. Interest (if any)		
4. Wages		
5. Taxes		
6. Utilities		
7. Miscellaneous		
Sub-Total		
Total		

CASH AVAILABILITY	SOURCE	AMOUNT

CHART 3-A. FINANCIAL PLAN

Facilities include your base of operations (shop, store, or factory), exclusive of equipment, tools, or inventory. If you can operate out of your home, the cash required to get into a shop or facility can be zero. If you are starting a restaurant, you will probably have to pay an initial fee when you sign a lease, even if you pay only the first and last months' rent. Any changes made to a facility before you can open fall into this category too.

Take the restaurant again as an example. Space rental includes no funds for installing equipment for decoration, a sign out front, or built-ins. Whether you call stoves, sinks, counters, and booths equipment or facilities can be arbitrary. One useful determiner—if it is portable and can be carried away, it's equipment. Money for anything built-in, such as a lighted ceiling, plumbing for a dishwasher, and the like, is part of the initial facility. Depending on your type of business, initial facilities investment can be substantial. Some of this investment must be paid for in cash—plumbers, carpenter labor for rearranging cabinets, partitions, etc. To pay for other parts you invest "sweat equity" by painting the place yourself, installing new floor tile—even installing your own cabinets, partitions, counters, etc. Here you must consider the rent paid during the added time it actually requires you to get the facility ready for operation.

Equipment—Ovens in a restaurant, tables and chairs, dishes—all of these items are used and reused rather than expended. You can either buy them or rent them. Consider both alternatives in your Financial Plan. Two factors govern your decision to rent or buy—

> —*Cost of rental vs. buying.* You figure your rental cost penalty (and rental will usually cost more than buying outright) by totaling the annual cost for monthly rentals. Compare this cost to the interest you would pay if you bought the equipment. For example, suppose a used oven for a restaurant cost $1,000. Or, you can rent the oven for $120 per month. Over the year, rental payments total $1,440. Compare the annual rental ($1,440) to the cost of borrowing the $1,000 at 12 percent interest. Your cost—$120 for the year, assuming no payment on the loan principal. The difference between $440 and $120 or $320 represents the penalty you pay for renting vs. buying.

—Cash available. Despite many obvious advantages of buying your equipment, you will probably not have enough cash to buy what you need. So, you rent—and the penalty becomes another of those costs of under-capitalization. Renting vs. buying also reduces start-up risks. But, you need to know the difference in costs between renting and buying so that you can assess relative penalties. Compute totals on both bases—rent and buy—and enter these amounts on your Financial Plan.

Inventory—Some businesses, such as a retail clothing store, depend heavily on stocking enough variety and sizes of each item to serve customers. Too little inventory turns customers away—and they don't come back. An excessive inventory, on the other hand, strains your start-up finances and depresses prof-its as a Return on Investment (ROI). The kind of business you start, your competition, your experience, and how much money you can raise all affect the level of your inventory.

Legal, advertising and promotion, and other miscellaneous items will vary widely according to your kind of business and whether you start small or go all-out at the beginning. But they all cost money, and possibly there are others you should know about that are not listed in Chart 3-A.

Operating expenses

These are recurring items that continue as your business continues. The most obvious ones are noted in Chart 3-B.

Again, consider each item in turn—

Cost of goods sold may be small in a service business, such as TV repairing, or a sizable portion of sales, as in a restaurant or a retail store. In a drive-in restaurant, for example, cost of goods sold covers all of the food supplies, plus the paper cups, napkins, and disposable items used in the serving of food,

	Monthly												Annual	
	1	2	3	4	5	6	7	8	9	10	11	12	Total	%
SALES														
COST OF GOODS SOLD Purchased Goods Labor														
Sub-Total														
OVERHEAD Rent Sales Expense Interest Repairs Equipment Depreciation Taxes														
Sub-Total														
PROFITS (LOSSES) RETURN ON INVESTMENT PERCENT OF SALES														

CHART 3-B. OPERATING PLAN

54

and direct labor. In a TV repair service, only the parts replaced are included and the major cost accrues as wages (yours or a helper's). Costs of goods sold vary directly with the volume of sales.

Rent and equipment-leasing fees are payable monthly and change very little relative to volume.

Interest on invested capital, loans, etc. must be considered as an operating expense. Such interest payments are directly chargeable against income in computing taxes.

Wages can be considered partially variable and partially fixed relative to business volume. One crew size can handle a minimum or maximum number of customers. You can change the number of employees for each limit—but not much in between. Wages include fringe benefits and your contribution to Social Security collections, plus any state assessments for a variety of services.

Taxes include sales taxes, income taxes, and the myriad of other items, from a Business and Occupation levy to annual licenses and permits.

Utilities include water, gas for heating, rubbish removal, electricity, telephone, and sewer.

Miscellaneous expenses include everything not specified in the others, such as insurance, legal fees, accounting services, repairs, etc.

Your operating expenses are likely to vary considerably between your first, sixth, and twelfth months. Therefore, don't consider only the expenses for one month's operations in your Cash Requirements. Instead, develop your Operating Plan for a full year. Chart 3-B defines the same elements noted in your operating expense plan, but extends them for the full year. You need to estimate, as best you can, operating revenues you can expect beyond the start-up period. For example, if your Operating Plan estimates a loss for the first three months, you must provide for that amount of cash—or equivalent—in your start-up Financial Plan. Under any circumstances, you should estimate the capital required for at least the first month's operations. You may substitute unpaid family labor as free. Unless you allocate a reasonable cost to this investment of labor by you, your spouse, or older children, you cannot calculate your real cost of doing business or true profitability. Consider unpaid family labor at no cost only to reduce cash requirements during the initial start-up.

Accumulating the capital needed

Cash Requirements, one part of your Financial Plan, defines how much cash you need. Now, where can you find the cash? Following are the usual sources—

Personal resources—Savings still form the first choice for funds to start a new business. Teamwork, with a wife working to save money to start a business instead of improving the family's standard of living (for the short run), accumulates funds faster than prying dollars out of a single paycheck. A moonlight job helps to build up savings quickly. Personal savings are important in any financing plan because bankers look at your investment in detail—unless you are fully committed, a banker will not ordinarily consider investing his bank's funds. In addition to personal savings, consider refinancing your home mortgage, selling some of your assets (expensive car, boat, trailer, a vacation home, rental house, etc.), borrowing on your insurance policy, or selling stocks acquired in the past (a form of personal savings).

Loans from outside sources—Banks remain the first choice for short-term capital—three months to a year. Whether you decide to borrow from a bank or not, talk with a loan officer anyway. You get an outsider's scrutiny of your plan without paying a consultant's fee. A banker will insist on details—your Financial Plan in developed written form for a starter. You will be amazed at the kinds of information a banker will insist on knowing before he puts money into your business—so be prepared. The discipline of applying for and backing up your requests for a loan can pay off handsomely—even if it turns out that your best bet is not to start your business. Hard-nosed advice at the beginning could head off many impending business failures—possibly yours. Banks supply the following kinds of funds—

—*Commercial loans* for specific periods—usually 30, 60, 90, or 120 days. Use these funds for short-term variations in volume; for example, to finance the purchase of an extra stock of toys for the Christmas season. Interest costs are simple to figure and vary according to risk, size of loan, condition of the money market, and your use of the funds.

—*Installment loans*—usually for longer periods than commercial loans, possibly for up to five years. Installment loans work much like a loan you take out to buy a car. Interest and a part of the principal are paid back each month. At the end of the period, you will have paid back the loan and all interest due in regular installments. Commercial loans, in comparison, are paid in full at the end of each period. Interest may be discounted (paid at the beginning) or added on at the end.

—*Term loans* may extend even longer than installment loans. If you can get a term loan, it becomes part of your long-term capital. Banks will require collateral—and some will insist on a regular review of your operations— possibly even a director on your board if your company is a corporation.

—*Special purpose loans*—to finance accounts receivable, warehouse receipts for stock, equipment leases, etc.

—*Line of credit* denotes a bank's willingness to lend you business money as needed up to a defined limit. You borrow and pay interest on the money as you need it without a new application each time. Usually, a line of credit is limited to well-established businesses rather than a new entry.

—*Participation loans* combine a loan of money with some other kind of financing—a loan from the Small Business Administration, equity investment by a Small Business Investment Company (SBIC), a nonprofit foundation, or a business-aiding group. Participation loans usually result from special situations—and always from detailed and special planning.

Loans from special sources—Specialized financial services provide funds for specific purposes, such as—

—*Factors* who advance money against accounts receivable. A factor may buy your accounts receivable at a discount. The factor collects from your customers, assumes the credit risk, and charges you a fee for his services. Depending on your type of business, and your need for capital, your credit and collection management abilities, and the condition of business, factoring can aid your business. Generally, factoring increases the cost of money compared to a straight bank loan—but you get additional services.

—*Small Business Administration loans* if participation loans (see above) or a guaranteed loan are not available. The SBA loans money directly only when money is not available elsewhere and your credit meets SBA requirements. The SBA loans money for as long as five years at reasonable rates against various types of collateral—land, buildings or equipment, warehouse receipts, chattels, or personal endorsements. Your best bet, if you believe you might qualify for a SBA loan, is to visit one of the SBA field offices.

Sell stock or equity in your company or proprietorship. Check with your state securities department if you intend to sell shares only within one state. The Securities and Exchange Commission gets involved if you intend a wide distribution of stock. However, you can sell limited amounts of stock to a few investors without registering the stock. Sale of an interest in an unincorporated business falls outside the jurisdiction of these security watchdog agencies. However, if your business is technically oriented, it offers considerable profit potential. Since you need several hundred thousand dollars of long-term equity capital, you might consider a public stock offering. If you do, get competent help from an experienced underwriter. The details of such a stock offering are beyond the scope of this book.

More practical is the sale of stock to one of the SBIC's. These Small Business Investment Companies are regulated and licensed by the Small Business Administration and sometimes borrow money from the SBA. Ordinarily, the SBIC sells its own stock to raise funds for investing in new, high-risk companies. SBIC's can invest in a corporation for a stock (equity) interest. They also loan money to individual proprietorships. Sometimes they do both—buy stock and loan money—to a corporation. Most SBIC's prefer investing in a new company in exchange for stock which they hope will grow in value and provide capital gains rather than simple interest on loans. When an SBIC takes an equity position, it also takes an active role in the company management—particularly financial management. Access to such professional assistance may be worth more to you and your business than the loan or investment—so, don't overlook these possibilities. Contact your banker or Chamber of Commerce for leads to SBIC'S in your community.

Local and state development funds specialize in financing small, starting businesses. The Southeastern Pennsylvania Development Fund, one of the sponsors of the Regional Development Laboratory in Philadelphia operates specifically to aid new companies or firms with loans and financial counsel. Your state's Department of Commerce or your local Chamber of Commerce can help you contact a new business development fund in your community.

Limited partnerships enable you to raise money from many investors much like the sale of stock. For many uses, mainly in real estate transactions, limited partnerships offer tax-shelter benefits for investors that are not available to stock purchasers. If you operate in the real estate field, check the possibilities of organizing a syndicate of general and limited partners to acquire and/or operate property. Leverage and depreciation affect earnings, so that partners receive more spendable tax-free income than from many stock investments. States regulate the formation and operation of limited partnerships closely to protect public investors. Since these state regulations vary widely, look into the specifics for your state if your business involves real estate. Limited partnerships can be a large and valuable source of funds when conditions are "right."

HOW TO SCRATCH UP THE MONEY YOU NEED

Your Financial Plan highlights the gap between the money you need and the funds you can raise (your own plus what you can borrow). Even if you scrape up the bare minimum, you should have access to more money—just in case. In franchises, for example, note the minimum amount of capital required—with emphasis on MINIMUM. Whether for your own business or a franchise, you'll probably need more money than you think—experience proves it. If you're typical, you will underestimate money requirements; either because from your inexperience you estimate low or forget, or in your enthusiasm and excitement to get started you skip lightly over money problems. One word of caution at this point—DON'T underestimate money needs. Face up to your capital requirements squarely—*before* you spend your capital resources—not AFTER, when you desperately need more money to continue. When an honest gap between cash available and cash required exists, try the following ideas.

Collect your sweat equity

Time and effort can sometimes substitute for cash. For example, Arnie Carriloni bought a used pizza baking oven for 20 percent as much as the cost of a new one. He completely rebuilt the oven in his spare time while he planned ahead. Even while rebuilding the oven, he was not committed to opening his pizza place. He could have sold the rebuilt oven at a profit. But, by investing a small amount of cash, plus a bundle of time and engineering know-how, he reduced his cash requirements. Other ideas you may use to develop sweat equity are—

Scrounge low-cost materials for remodeling a shop, store, or other facility. Look for sources for cut-rate paint, building materials, used plumbing, etc.

Barter your expertise, time, and effort for something you need. Harriet B. traded several of her best pots for photographs from a professional. Then, she used the photos to develop promotional literature that helped her sell to stores. Her craft products became trading material—better than money when dealing with a creative photographer. A large space in a booming shopping center was to be cut up into three stores. So, Oscar H., a part-time carpenter, made a deal. He built the partitions, installed a new ceiling, new doors, and other changes necessary to make each of the business spaces self-sufficient. In exchange, Oscar obtained the lease for one of the spaces rent-free for a year—and the developer saved more than contractor estimates.

Buy used tools and equipment

One of the most underrated resources in our country is the used market for practically everything—from salvaged building materials, to furniture, to hardware. When Frank Sweeney decided to lease a service station, he needed tools—so he watched the classified ads and shopped the used equipment market. By picking and choosing, he accumulated a full chest of wrenches plus specialized tools—and a full range of auto diagnostic and tune-up equipment for about 25 percent of the cost if he had purchased them all new. Practically anything is available used. Sometimes you need to refurbish it before use—a good application of sweat equity. Don and Janis P. took on a whole roomful of badly used restaurant booths and tables. The pieces were replaced during renovation of a restaurant. Together Don and Janis recovered each of the cushioned booth seats; Don stripped off the old plastic laminate and glued on new tops for the tables. When they finished, they had equipment worth $4,000 new for only $600 in materials plus just under 250 hours between them.

Tap new sources for funds

Play the little-bit game—raise some of the money you need by borrowing in $10 or $25 amounts. You'll find borrowing $25 from ten friends, relatives, or associates easier than borrowing $250 from one friend. You might also sell future goods or services at a discount—$25 gift or merchandise certificates at a 20 percent discount. In addition to raising money from your friends and relatives by loans or sales of goods or services, consider these possible sources—

Credit union—If you plan to continue working at your regular job and start your new business moonlighting, borrow from your company credit union—or one of the other credit unions you may have access to.

Lodge, union, or pension funds—Local administration of these funds often makes them available to friends—but only as prudent investments. You can expect the same hard-nosed scrutiny from a fund manager as from a bank loan officer.

Private investors—Your banker, or some other friend within the big business clique, might put you next to an individual with funds available for special situations—like your new business. Robertson Aircraft, for example, modified a special airplane in exchange for working capital during its early stages. Individuals may insist on a "piece of the business" as well as interest on their money. But, these individuals will put up risk capital when the opportunities appear ripe for a major gain. Just watch your step and don't give up an excessive interest in your business for a few bucks.

MONEY TO EXPAND YOUR BUSINESS

Once you get your business under way—sales progressing satisfactorily, income increasing, most of your borrowed capital paid back, and profits over and above your salary coming in regularly—what next? You'd like to expand your business. Growth doesn't just happen. Successful businesses plan for growth—building and selling new products, opening a new store, expanding the line of products sold. Chart 3-C depicts a general-purpose look five years ahead with a rising sales volume projected. Note that the uppermost sales volume is not defined. What new product or service must you develop to keep the sales

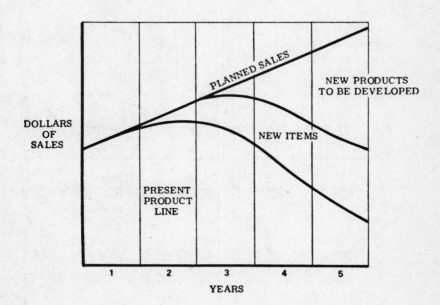

CHART 3-C

volume expanding? As older products and services decline, they must be continually replaced with new ones. You face two problems in long-range planning—

- Where will the added sales come from?
- Where will the funds needed to expand the sales come from?

Planning works effectively even if you are a service-station operator. Examine your options—stay open longer hours; add a second or third lift to increase grease, oil change, and the repair capacity; expand tire business aggressively; or advertise and promote greater sales with coupons, games, or other means. Your business grows because you plan for growth—then put your plan into action.

Planning your capital requirements follows the general scheme shown in Chart 3-D. Note the five-year look ahead. Begin with Gross Sales for each product line as a reference. Follow through with the major elements necessary to achieve your planned growth of sales—

YEAR AHEAD

ITEM	1	2	3	4	5
GROSS SALES					
PRODUCT A					
PRODUCT B					
PRODUCT C					
OTHERS					
TOTAL					

CHART 3-D. FIVE-YEAR PLAN

YEAR AHEAD	1	2	3	4	5
CAPITAL REQ'D					
PROD. DEV.					
FACILITIES					
PERSONNEL					
ACCTS. REC.					
INVENTORY					
SALES PROM.					
OTHER					
—					
—					
SUB-TOTAL					
CAPITAL AVAIL.					
DEPRECIATION					
RET. EARNINGS					
SUB-TOTAL					
INVEST. REQ'D					
LOANS					
EQUITY					
OTHER					

CHART 3-D. FIVE-YEAR PLAN (continued)

- Product development calls for expenditures ahead of sales to try new ideas, test their market acceptance, develop manufacturing or selling techniques—everything necessary to develop new or improved business opportunities to expand sales volume.

- Facilities are those long-range expenses necessary to produce new products or more of the old line—factory space, sales branches, laboratory facilities, etc.

- Personnel needs go up with increased sales. So, you must plan for recruiting and training new people.

- Accounts receivable grow as business volume expands—sometimes at an increased rate compared to present volume.

- Inventory of parts in work or in finished stores increases with growth in sales—so money must be available to finance higher inventory volume.

- Sales promotion—advertising, exhibits, personal sales forces—all are needed to reach projected sales growth, and they all require additional money.

- Other costs will depend on your kind of business—management training, transportation costs, etc.

Your job in long-range planning is to project growth in sales along with the capital and labor required to achieve that growth. Part of the cash for growth investment can come from depreciation allowances and retained earnings. When you determine how much additional capital you need each year, you can arrange to acquire the funds through a variety of means—

Loans may be desirable to retain your share of control and stock (if your company is a corporation). With a profitable operating record, loans for expansion are relatively easy to obtain at reasonable rates.

Equity financing through a sale of stock to the public may be a way to achieve two goals: (1) raise the money you need for expansion, and (2) sell a portion of your interest in the company for a major capital gain that puts more spendable cash in your own pocket.

Other means—a merger with another company, a sale of bonds to an insurance company, or a sale-leaseback of certain facilities owned in part or in full by your company.

Acquiring the funds you need for expansion will be easier than raising funds to start your business—particularly if you develop a detailed, five-year look ahead along the lines of Chart 3-D.

4

How You Can Tap the Money
Sources of the Wealthy

As a fledgling business person, you probably have the
basic knowledge needed to keep records which separate your
gains from your losses. These are elementary essentials. However, no matter how clever you are about money matters, it is
likely that you will need financing at some stage of your
business.

It takes money to expand, to grow, to enlarge your base of
operation. But don't let the word finance scare you. Borrowing
money isn't the awesome and frightening process some people
have painted it. In this chapter you will learn some Wealth-
Building Secrets to help you borrow money and profit right
from the beginning.

From Marian Behan Hammer, *The Complete Handbook of How to
Start and Run a Money-Making Business in Your Home* (West Nyack, N.Y.,
Parker Publishing Company, Inc., 1975)

EXPLORING YOUR SOURCES OF CAPITAL

There are some business ventures which can be started with no investment whatsoever, utilizing instead, a talent, a skill, or materials which you already possess. There are also those endeavors which require some small amount of capital, and there are those for which thousands of dollars are required. However, even for those ventures which require no money outlay at the start, as the business progresses, availability of money sometimes becomes essential. Now where do you get the money you need?

As suggested in the previous chapter, your first source of capital could be *your own pocket.* If you are starting on a small scale, you might possibly have enough money on hand to buy the materials and equipment you will need to put yourself in business. This can be money from a personal savings account, from stocks and bonds, or from an insurance policy. However, you will need more than this "starting" money. It is wise to keep in mind that every business needs capital for two reasons.

1. You need money for your initial business plunge.

2. You need money to use as your business progresses.

The first will take care of fixed assets, such as equipment or tools. The second, classified as working capital, will be needed for supplies, paying wages, extending credit, and other day-to-day operating expenses, plus marketing and advertising expenses.

Because it is very important for you as a new business person to have sufficient capital on hand, if you aren't able to finance yourself there are several other places to turn for financial help. One was described in the previous chapter as SEM (Somebody Else's Money). This doesn't mean, however, that you approach anyone with the idea of a handout or a personal loan. You must be prepared to offer a percentage of your business, perhaps a partnership or a corporation deal. Such an arrangement means that you must work with someone else and share the control of the business with him. Even though he may be a "silent" partner, you must be prepared for his recommendations and offers of advice in every aspect of the business. However, if you're not willing to take someone into your business just to obtain capital, there are other places to look.

There are economic opportunity loans available from the government. This type of loan makes it possible for the disadvantaged, who have the capability and the desire, to own their own business and to become part of the economic life of their community. Both prospective and established small businessmen may receive assistance under this program. It provides both financial and management assistance, with a maximum amount of $25,000 for up to 15 years.

To qualify for this program, an applicant must demonstrate the ability to operate a business successfully. There must be reasonable assurance that the loan can be repaid from the earnings of the business, and the applicant is expected to have some of his own assets invested. It is also required that his total income not be sufficient for his basic family needs, and that due to social or economic disadvantage he is denied the opportunity to acquire business financing through normal lending channels.

If you think you might qualify for this program, contact your SBA field office, or write to Small Business Administration, Office of Public Information, Washington, D.C. 20416.

Another area you might wish to investigate as a source of capital is the venture capitalists. These are individuals or organizations who are willing to lend money as an investment for themselves. If you deal with these people you might expect to pay a higher interest rate than on money obtained from a commercial bank. To ensure protection for yourself as well as the lender, make certain that all papers are drawn up by a reliable attorney.

Another source of capital for the advanced business is a loan through an insurance broker. A few insurance companies, such as the Prudential Insurance Company of America, make mortgage loans on commercial properties and others offer term loans such as you might obtain from a bank. This type of financing involves rather high interest rates, usually on a 12-year basis, and the companies which offer it are extremely selective, looking for businesses which return 20 percent or better on equity, and almost always requiring warrants or conversion privileges to obtain stock of the borrower company. However, it might pay you to investigate this source, if you can offer adequate security.

The business opportunity columns of your newspaper are another source of capital that can't be overlooked. For instance, the following ads appeared in a single recent issue of a major newspaper.

> Private investor financing consultant has clients with unlimited funds for worthwhile solid business proposals.

> Are you endowed with the ability but lacking sufficient capital or encouragement to proceed on your own? I can help finance and actively participate in a joint venture.

> Immediate cash available. Any worthwhile project anywhere in the U.S.

Advertised operations of this type range from the highly respectable down to outright loan sharks, so be especially careful with whom you deal, and what you sign.

Of all the sources frequently used by the beginning business person, *bank loans* still remain most popular. You will be well advised to consider bank financing, particularly since your local bank is anxious to provide financing for businesses within its service area and will tend to be liberal and helpful. The amount your bank can or will lend, depends to a large extent on what you, the borrower, have as capital.

WHAT YOU SHOULD KNOW ABOUT BORROWING

Some beginning business people can't understand why they are turned down when they apply for a loan at a lending institution, when others have no problem in obtaining a loan from the same source. They are also surprised to discover that there may be strings attached to their loan. It is important that before you approach anyone for a loan you know something about borrowing money.

One of the most important factors in obtaining a loan is to make sure your business is credit worthy. A bank or any other lending source wants to make loans to businesses which are solvent, profitable, and growing, or have the potential thereof.

A lender will also hesitate to lend money to you if you are vague about *how much you need* and for what purpose it is needed.

When seeking funds for a small business, bear in mind that your request or proposal is competing with all other applications. The attractiveness of any particular type of proposal depends on many factors in addition to the figure analysis. Some are personal, regional, or institutional preferences. There are also factors akin to fashion cycles.

Here are some questions to ask yourself before you ask for a loan.

1. What sort of person am I? As far as my business is concerned, am I reliable and do I have the knowledge and ability to make a go of it?

2. What am I going to do with the money and how much do I need? When starting a new business, one doesn't have the advantage of estimates based on previous inventories and accounts receivable. Therefore, your needs must be fairly accurate estimates.

3. Am I borrowing for the purchase of fixed assets or

working capital or both? Be sure to allow ample cash for your working capital; for instance, giving yourself lee-way to do special promotion work at the right times, and to keep your credit rating high.

4. When and how can I pay back the loan? Your business ability and the type of loan you are able to obtain may well be determined according to your answer to this question.

5. What is the outlook for business in general and for my business in particular?

Aside from answers to the above questions, there are other *questions the lender will want answered.*

As previously mentioned, your business can acquire capital from private and public financing. There are advantages to both. If your company is already of significant size in earnings and assets so as to be able to sell stock, some of the advantages of public financing are:

1. More lenient terms and less direct interference in the operation of the company.

2. The publicity that a registered public offering brings can be beneficial.

3. A lower cost of acquiring money.

However, if your business is just getting started, the largest source of financing available to you is private. It offers these advantages:

1. Money can be obtained more quickly than through stock issue.

2. It costs less because there are no registration and under-writing expenses.

3. If you wish to change business practices or make adjust-ments in your business, you have only yourself or a

partner to deal with, rather than needing the vote of all the stockholders.

4. If your first source of capital is satisfied, a second loan can be easily negotiated.

5. There is no need to disclose your operating figures to the public and your competitors.

MATCHING THE SOURCE OF YOUR CAPITAL WITH YOUR NEED

When you set out to borrow money it is important to match the source of your capital with your need. The purpose for which the funds are to be used and the way you intend to repay the debt are important factors to be considered. Therefore, be sure you choose a lending institution appropriate for you. Each has its own policies and standards. Don't borrow from your old family banker, for instance, just because your family has been banking with him for years. Do a bit of scouting first to see where you can get the best deal.

Suppose you need *a short-term loan* for inventory purposes. You intend to repay the debt as soon as your inventory is complete and has been converted into salable merchandise. In this case, the lender expects his loan to be repaid within a short period of time, as soon as its purpose has been served and usually no longer than three to six months. Such money is granted either on your general credit reputation with an unsecured loan or on a secured loan—against collateral.

The *unsecured loan* is the most frequently used method of obtaining funds and represents a loan from a commercial bank. You are not required to put up any collateral, but are granted the loan on your credit reference.

A *secured loan,* on the other hand, involves a pledge of some or all of your assets. This is the largest source of financing available to you and can be obtained from banks, individuals, and insurance companies. Acceptable collateral would be real estate, stock, capital equipment, inventory, and accounts receivable.

For example, using private stock as collateral, Ted O'Keefe secured a loan of $1,500 to enlarge his small cement sculpture business. With the loan he was able to buy new molds and another cement mixer (used), and thereby take advantage of a large order placed by a local seed store owner. This exposure led to more and bigger orders which enabled him to pay back his loan in 90 days.

Term-borrowing is another way to acquire money. This is money which you plan to pay back over a long period of time. It can be broken down into two forms:

1. Intermediate, which consists of loans longer than 1 year, but less than 5 years.
2. Loans for more than 5 years.

Most people pay back a term loan in periodic installments from earnings. For example, four years ago, Sophie Lewis borrowed $8,000 from her banker to expand her arts and crafts business operation. The loan was to be repaid in monthly payments over a 10-year period. Now, in her enlarged building, she not only offers classes in arts and crafts, but has many "home crafted" articles for sale which she imports from all parts of the country. Because this new attraction adds greatly to her income, she feels confident that her debt will easily be paid off in accordance with her agreement.

Equity capital is money you don't have to repay. But you must sell a part interest in your business to obtain it. If your company is a going concern, people will be willing to risk their money in the purchase of stock. They are interested in potential income rather than in an immediate return on their investment. However, this is seldom a practical route for the beginning business.

KNOWING ABOUT BANK LOANS

New business people often feel ill-at-ease when dealing with banks. Frequently their experience with them and their knowledge of how they operate is limited to the use of a personal checking or savings account. However, most banks offer a wide variety of services of value to the business person. Aside from business loans, these can include:

Credit references on customers

Check certification

Payment of freight invoices

Payroll accounting services

Discounting customers' accounts and notes payable

Safe deposit boxes

Night depositories

Perhaps the bank you deal with at present is as good as any other, and can offer you the services necessary for your business. However, before making a final decision, here are 12 pointers to help you choose the right bank.

1. If possible, choose a bank with knowledge of your type of business. Such knowledge can better help them understand and evaluate your business needs.
2. Choose a progressive bank. Some banks are more interested in loans for new products and services than are others.
3. Choose a bank convenient to your business. This not only lessens the risk involved in transporting cash, but acquaints you with another businessman in your neighborhood—your banker—who has faith in the future of your community and will be willing to invest in it.

4. Check the size of a bank. Usually a convenient branch bank can offer you all the services of its main office, or a small bank can draw on the resources of a larger bank.

5. Choose a bank whose officers are available for consultation when you need it. Your choice of a bank is best made when you first start out in business. However, if you discover, as Sophie Lewis did after she had been in her arts and craft business for several years, that your current bank doesn't offer you all it should, it's time to change. Mrs. Lewis visited several banking establishments in her vicinity and talked with the president of each one. In locating the one that best fulfilled her needs, she used all of the pointers listed above as well as those which follow.

6. Choose a bank used by a number of potential customers, where check clearance will be quickly available to you.

7. Choose a bank that is willing to furnish you with the information you need concerning customer credit.

8. Choose a bank that makes all types of loans available.

9. Choose a bank that doesn't take long to have a loan approved.

10. Check on the type and amount of collateral required for loans.

11. Check on repayment terms.

12. Check to see if you must maintain certain balances before the bank will grant you a loan.

Figure 4-A is an example of a personal financial statement, similar to that which you will be asked to fill out when applying for a bank loan.

When you have satisfied yourself that you have found the right bank, there are certain things your bank will want to know

APPLICATION FOR LOAN

Source

Amount of Note $		No. Inst.

Previous Yes ☐ No ☐ Dept.

Experience

| Balance $ | | Amount Inst. $ | | Final Inst. $ |

PRINT FULL NAME — Last Name — First Name — Initial — Draft Status — Rating — Age — M ☐ S ☐ Widower ☐ Widow ☐

First Inst. Due

Name of Spouse — Age — No. of Dependents — Phone No.

ACCOUNT NO.

CODE

Print MAIL Address — R. F. D. Directions — Under Remarks — How Long

Amount Loaned $

Residence Address — Explain Under Remarks — How Long

Rate %

Former Address — How Long

Interest $

Nearest Relative — Relationship — Address — City — State

Credit Life Ins. $

Wife's Nearest Relative — Relationship — Address — City — State

Minimum Service Charge $

Amount of Note $

Occupation — Firm Name — How Long — Former Employer — How Long

DISBURSEMENT

Own Home Yes ☐ No ☐ — Rent or Mo. Pmt. $ — Bal. on Mtg. $ — Real Estate Value $ — Landlord's Name and Address — Bank With — Checking ☐ Savings ☐

To Borrower $

Credit References — Loan Value

To Dealer $

1. — Motor Vehicle — Make — Description — Yes ☐ No ☐ $ Mtg.

To $

19......... — Yes ☐ No ☐ $ Mtg.

To $

19......... — 2. 3.

To $

If Auto Loan – Insured With — Monthly Income

To $

The Following Constitute All Debts and Obligations Owed by Me/Us:

To Whom Owed	Nature of Debt	Balance Due	Monthly Payment
		$	$
		$	$
		$	$
		$	$
	TOTAL $		

To $

Total Credits $

Remarks:

I hereby certify that all these statements are true and are made for the purpose of obtaining a loan for $........ from The Peoples-Merchants Trust Co. and I authorize your Bank to obtain any information that you require concerning the statements in this application.

DATE _____ 19 ____   SIGN HERE _____

Approved by

PMT-490

FIGURE 4-A

about you. On your first visit you might bring a prospectus estimating expected sales, expenses, and anticipated profits. Don't try to pad the financial facts about your business. They are best placed out in the open for you and your banker to examine. This mutual frankness will help to build your reputation for good character integrity, and since bankers, like lawyers and doctors, have a code of ethics, the information will be kept confidential.

The three pointers listed below will help you to get faster and better service from your bank.

Explain your plans freely, even inviting your banker to your home to show him your place of operation.

Tell him about your source of materials and other supplies.

Explain your business experience and the operating techniques you plan to use.

In building a strong relationship with your bank, *getting to know your banker pays off.* Jon Maxwell's banker, Fred Hanns, is not only a business associate but a friend as well, a relationship which began when the two men served together on a civic affairs committee. As a friend, Fred was in on the ground floor of Jon's nursery business, taking a personal interest and steering him to many shortcuts when he was in need of service from the bank. For instance, when Jon needs a quick credit reference, he can ask Fred for information over the phone.

Once you have established a rapport with your banker, it is important that you *keep a good credit rating.* The following pointers will help you.

1. Make sure your accounting system is accurate.
2. At all times know the cost of offering your product or service to the consumer, of selling, and maintaining it.
3. Don't allow your bank accounts to become accidentally overdrawn.

4. Don't skimp on the amount of money you borrow to run your business, but be sure to pay it back with interest when it is due.

5. Don't abuse your credit by using money borrowed from the bank for any purpose except that for which it was loaned to you.

CHECKING ON YOUR COLLATERAL

When it comes to lending money, there are few individuals or institutions that are willing to take unnecessary risks. This is especially true of banks. Therefore, even when dealing with a bank at which you are well known, don't feel offended if you are asked for some type of collateral.

When requesting a loan from a bank where you have maintained a long standing account, your signature as security may be the only necessary requirement. However, in most cases, the bank will expect you to put up something else of value as assurance that the money will be repaid.

A *chattel mortgage loan* is one way to obtain the money you need. Sometimes you can get a loan by assigning your *life insurance policy* to the bank. Another kind of collateral, which can be assigned to the bank, is your savings account. In such cases, an assignment statement must be signed by you and your passbook held by the bank. If your savings are in a different bank, it will be noted in their records that the account is being held as collateral for the lender bank.

Real estate is another form of collateral which is acceptable for loan purposes. If you own property you wish to use in this way, your bank will need the following information.

Location of the real estate

What it consists of as regards buildings and land

The foreclosure value

The type and amount of insurance you now carry on the property

If you don't wish to offer any of the above as collateral, there are other ways to avail yourself of a loan. Perhaps you might make use of a co-maker, an endorser, or a guarantor. These are people who can bolster your credit by signing a note with you. They make themselves liable for the note they sign should you fail to pay your debt.

Established businesses often obtain money on their accounts receivable, although this is not a probable source of collateral for the person who is starting a new business. However, if you have advance orders for your product or service it is not impossible.

A bank may take accounts receivable on a notification or a non-notification plan. Under the first, the customer is informed by the bank that his account has been assigned to it and he is asked to pay the bank. The other plan allows your customer to continue to pay you, and you in turn pay the bank.

If you own stocks and bonds, these can also be used for collateral, but they must be marketable. As a protection against declines in the market value, banks usually lend no more than 75 percent of the market value of high grade stock. On Federal Government or municipal bonds, they may be willing to lend 90 percent or more of the market value.

HOW LENDERS' LIMITATIONS CAN
AFFECT YOUR BUSINESS

A lending party, whether an individual or a bank, is not just interested in having a loan repaid. It is also interested in the borrower who has a healthy profit-making business. Therefore, even though they may require collateral for a loan, they set loan limitations and restrictions to protect themselves against unnecessary risk and against poor management practices by their borrowers. Sometimes these lenders' limitations can affect your business, although not always adversely.

Why are you required to sign *a loan agreement?* This is a

document which covers or refers to all the terms and conditions of the loan. The reasons for such an agreement are twofold.

1. They protect the lender's position as a creditor.
2. They assure the lender of repayment according to the terms.

Negative covenants in the agreement restrict the borrower from acting in certain capacities without the lender's approval. For example: he can't add to his debt, such as applying for another loan from another source.

On the other hand, *positive covenants* spell out things the borrower must do. Examples:

He must maintain a minimum net working capital.

He must carry adequate insurance.

He must repay the loan according to the terms of the agreement.

He must supply the lender with financial statement and reports.

Be sure to thrash out the lending terms of an agreement *before you sign.* Although loan agreements can be amended from time to time, or certain provisions may be waived from one year to the next with the consent of the lender, it is always wise to check them out carefully beforehand. Ask to see the papers in advance of the closing date and get the advice of your associates and outside advisors. Try to get terms that you know you can live with a year from now as well as at the present time. Often a legitimate lender will give some if you point out that a certain term or terms will be difficult to fulfill.

Banks and other lending institutions ask that you sign a loan application, in duplicate, before advancing you a loan. Some applications are more detailed than others, necessitating more knowledge about the applicant. Figure 4-B represents a simple statement such as might be required by most banks.

LOAN APPLICATION

Date _____

OFFICE: 01 - Canton – 02 - Massillon – 03 - Brewster – 04 - Belden – 05 - 30th Street – 06 - North Canton
☐   New   ☐   Renewal

BORROWER	COSIGNER (S)
NAME:	NAME:
ADDRESS:	ADDRESS:
TELEPHONE:	TELEPHONE:
OCCUPATION:	OCCUPATION:

Amount applied for _____ Rate _____

If Renewal:
Original Date: _____

Total (including this application) owed Bank _____

Original Amt.: _____

TYPE OF LOAN:

☐   Secured Demand   ☐   Unsecured Demand
☐   Secured Time (30, 60, 90 day)   ☐   Unsecured Time (30, 60, 90 day)
☐   Secured Term (Over 365 day)   ☐   Unsecured Term (Over 365 day)
☐   Secured (Minimum Charge)   ☐   Unsecured (Minimum Charge)

PURPOSE OF LOAN: Business ☐   Purchase Securities ☐   Personal ☐
_____
_____
_____

PAYMENT PROGRAM: PAYMENT FREQUENCY:

☐   Pay in Full at Maturity   ☐   Stated Payments to be Made Monthly
☐   Renewals Permissible at Maturity   ☐   Stated Payments to be Made Quarterly
☐   Renewals Permitted with Reduction of Principle   ☐   Stated Payments to be Made Annually
☐   Disposition to be Discussed with Loan Officer   ☐   Stated Payments to be Made Irregularly

Payment Amount _____   Includes Interest ☐   Excludes Interest ☐

Description of Security: _____
_____

Statement Date: _____   Maturity Date: _____

APPLICANT ALSO HAS: Signature of Borrower and Cosigner:

☐   Time Deposits   Amount _____   Mr. _____

☐   Demand Deposits   Amount _____   Miss/Mrs. _____

☐   Installment Loans   Amount _____   Mr. _____

☐   Other Commercial Loans   Amount _____   Miss/Mrs. _____

☐   Trust

☐   Safe Deposit Box   Officer _____

☐   Master Charge   Additional Comments on Reverse:
                                                ☐   Yes   ☐   No
☐   Computer Application

☐   Other (Explain)   Committee Action:

PMT-622 Rev. 7/72

FIGURE 4-B

For more information on financing your beginning business, the following booklets can be obtained *free* from field offices and Washington headquarters of the Small Business Administration, Washington, D.C.

Loan Sources in the Federal Government—Management Aid #52.

The ABC's of Borrowing—Management Aid #170.

Building Strong Relations with Your Bank—Management Aid #107.

Is Your Cash Supply Adequate?—Management Aid #174.

5

How to Get a Million Dollars Worth of Free Help from the Top People

The chances are you are reading this book because you want to build something for yourself—either a part-time venture or a full-time business that will give you wealth and independence. In either case, you are probably a pretty independent person. You hesitate to ask for favors. You are the kind of person who has the spirit and drive to get things done and you like to do them by yourself. And, as such, you probably are reluctant to ask others for help when you need it. But, before you take on all of the problems yourself, read this story of a man who was fiercely independent, but who was able to use the best promotional brains in the country without charge or obligation.

Warren H. was a salesman for a large company. He was doing reasonably well, but he knew that if he was ever going to make it really big, it would not be through the ranks of the

From Herbert Holtje and John Stockwell, *How to Borrow Everything You Need to Build a Great Personal Fortune* (West Nyack, N.Y., Parker Publishing Company, Inc., 1974)

company that was giving him his bread and butter as a salesman. And, he knew that he was short on capital, but long on ideas. In fact, Warren did develop a commercial use for waste material that was thrown away daily by his employer.

Before he thought of going into business for himself, Warren had told his boss about the idea and all he got for his trouble was a laugh. Warren's boss had very little imagination, and he was not interested in having one of his subordinates come up with an idea that he should have developed himself. Warren immediately recognized that he was up against a stone wall. His boss would not give him the recognition he needed and there was no place to go in the company as long as he worked for this unreasonable man.

GETTING THOUSANDS OF DOLLARS WORTH OF PUBLICITY—FREE

Warren decided that he would try to start a part-time venture, with an eye to turning it into a full-time business when the volume was sufficient. But, he didn't have the money to promote it nationally.

Warren used one of the most important Wealth-Building Secrets. He got his message to just about every industrial purchasing agent (his main market), without spending a cent for advertising, by preparing a simple photo of his product, in an inexpensively printed news release, and sending it to the editors of many trade magazines. Warren did this, and within a few months, nine major industrial magazines carried small articles and pictures of his product. In six more months, Warren was so busy that he had to quit his selling job to devote more time to his rapidly expanding business. From an operation in his basement, he now has a plant with thousands of square feet, a home with a swimming pool in the country, and is planning to build a beautiful vacation home on a small island in the Caribbean. And he owes this to his rocket-fast start with O.P.T.—Other People's

Talent. In this case, it was the time and talent of the magazine editors that got him on the road to success and independence.

USING O.P.T. TO BUILD SUCCESS

No matter how many times you have run across people who will kick you when you are down, there are just as many people who will lend you a hand when you have ideas and the drive to see them through. The editors in the story you just read were willing to do this, and because of them, Warren got thousands of dollars worth of free publicity for his idea. In fact, even now when Warren spends many thousands of dollars a year to advertise his greatly expanded line of products, he still leans heavily on the free publicity service offered by these helpful editors.

O.P.T., then, is a commodity like money—other people's money. You can use it and you can profit from it. You can get it free, you can get it in exchange for services, you can get it on speculation, but the important fact is that you *can* get it and you must use it if you are starting with limited capital.

FINDING O.P.T. EVERYWHERE

Perhaps you are conjuring up the picture of a greedy person who will lend a hand only to collect heavily from you at some later date. People like this do exist, but there are more than enough people who have been through the mill who are ready and willing to give you the help you need, with no strings attached. For example, in New York City, there is a group of retired business professionals who help small businessmen every day. The Executive Volunteer Corps, as they are known, is made up of such people. You will be surprised just how helpful people can be when you ask. For one thing, people like to think that others are turning to them because of their achievement

and stature. It means that they have arrived, that they are considered to be important people.

GETTING TOP EXECUTIVES TO GIVE YOU
THE ANSWERS

There is one man who regularly gets free, helpful advice
from top corporation executives. He found that when he asked
lesser management people for advice, they were often secretive
and jealous of their information and position. But, when he
asked the presidents of big companies, they were flattered by
the request. Try it and you will see how easy it is to get to see
top people. It's a lot more difficult to get to the lower managers,
and they seldom have the answers.

HOW O.P.T. CAN MULTIPLY YOUR
RESOURCES AND PROFITS

Consider for a minute a business that employs thousands
of people. Such a business has every kind of specialist available
on its staff, and these people are available to solve problems
whenever they come up. But, you are starting a business that,
for the time being, will employ no one but yourself. You will
do everything, if you find the time—and have the experience.
You will handle the bookkeeping . . . the advertising . . . the
manufacturing . . . the selling . . . the office details . . . and even
carry out the garbage when the can is full. Discouraged? Don't
be, because, if you follow this simple system, you can have all
of these things done for you at little or no cost.

One of the big mistakes most small businessmen make is to
try to be experts in every business operation. It can't be done,
and unless you have the money to pay for these professionals,
you will find yourself in trouble.

But, suppose you were able to find an accountant, an advertising man, an engineer, a salesman, and even an employment specialist—you would be able to tap Other People's Talent to build your business in half the time it would take alone. Consider just what it would cost to employ all of these people to do the work. And, imagine just what it would take to do all this work yourself. Is it any wonder so few new businesses survive?

As you should begin to see, by using Other People's Talent, you can virtually eliminate most of these problems, and you can get the kind of professional help that will assure your success.

HOW TO MAKE OTHER PEOPLE EAGER
TO WORK FOR YOU

You can stop making false starts on the path to wealth by carefully picking the brains of the professionals. It has been said that knowledge is power. No man can have all the knowledge needed to make a business a success. But, if he knows how to get other people to share their knowledge, this fact will be far more valuable than the combined skills of all the professionals helping him. And this is just what you are going to get in the pages of this chapter.

"Why," you might ask, "would anyone be willing to help me?"

"I have very little money."

"I'm not sure that my idea will work."

"I have a limited education."

"There is a lot of competition."

And thousands of other excuses.

Regardless of how many reasons you can muster, it is still possible to get the help of talented professionals for little or no cost. Here are just a few of the things you can do to guarantee that other people will want to help you.

Have a solid idea. This does not mean that the idea has to be completely original. After all, imagine how many hula hoops have been invented! But an old and successful idea, well thought out, is more likely to succeed than many dazzling, way-out schemes. For example, the simple idea of opening a store in an area where no stores like it exist has more chance of success than the once-in-a-million ideas that sometimes make the headlines. But, the idea must be sound, well researched, and carefully organized.

Have a positive mental attitude. If you are going to attract other people to help you, you must be able to show them that you have confidence in your ideas. Often, the difference between success and failure when the same idea is tried by two different people is the attitude they project to other people. When a man has confidence in what he is doing, success is obvious to the people around him. When he is unsure, people are also aware of it, and are often unwilling to take a chance, or even to offer free advice. Many people with sound, but very ordinary, ideas turned them into wild successes only because they had the kind of an outlook that said to people, "This is a winner—this will succeed." People like to bet on winners. You must adopt a winner's outlook.

Be aware of what other people want. When you seek the help, advice, and counsel of other people in your Wealth-Building activities, you must be aware of their own personal needs. For example, when you ask a person for advice, you are actually saying to him, "You, sir, are an expert and I am coming to you for help because I recognize your vast accomplishments." Of course, you would never use these actual words, but when you seek help from a person who has the background to offer the help, you are acknowledging his accomplishments. This makes the person feel important and he will do just about anything not to let you down.

Dangle the carrot. You may not be able to offer to pay for the accounting services you need. And, you may not be able to pay an advertising man to prepare a news release for you, but you can offer future rewards without giving your business away. If you have carefully thought out your plans, you will have some idea of just where your venture will be in a year—or two years—and you can tell these people that you will then be able to offer them active and financially rewarding contracts. For example, it is not uncommon for an accountant to offer his services to a prospective venture, if he believes in it, for the opportunity of handling the account when the business grows. You can, of course, do this with just about any of the other services you will need to start and operate your business. There are specific details on individual services you can tap, later in this chapter. But, in the meantime, remember, the offer of a future reward for some early professional assistance can be a very powerful inducement for the help you will need.

TAPPING THE PRIME SOURCE OF O.P.T.

Before you go looking for outside talent to tap for your venture, be sure to check on the talent bank you inherited—your family. Many people are afraid to get involved with their family in a business way; but, properly handled, a family can often supply most of the talent needed to get a business off the ground.

Many successful businesses owe their success to the early employment of a relative's talent. For example, Martin H. would never have made the success he did if it hadn't been for the fact that his brother had taken an accounting course in college. Mind you, his brother was not an accountant, but had only taken a few credits of accounting while majoring in economics.

Martin had started a small mail order business in his basement. He was selling office supplies and printed forms through the mail when his brother offered to take a look at the books. Martin was somewhat reluctant. First, because he was not anxious to let his brother know how he was doing; and second, because he thought that he was doing a good enough job by himself. After a review of the books and the botch that was made of the daily records, Martin's brother was able to put this business into the black quickly. Oddly enough, these brothers later joined forces in the business and today run a very successful mail order business.

You don't even have to rely on such sophisticated talent in your family. Consider the many husband-and-wife operations that make use of just about every member of the family. More often than not, the wife can type well enough to handle most of the correspondence. The kids can handle packing after school. And there are always enough relatives with the desire to earn a few dollars for part-time work. While this situation is ideal for starting a business, many husband-and-wife operations continue this way and make fortunes for an entire family.

DISCOVERING O.P.T. WITHIN WALKING DISTANCE OF YOUR HOME

Every neighborhood is a treasure trove of untapped talent: housewives looking to earn a few extra dollars; kids looking for after-school, part-time work; and even the men of the area hoping to pick up a few extra bucks for a Saturday job or to do a few hours of work during the weekday evenings.

Whatever you need, the chances are that the talent exists within a few blocks of you right now. And, even if you cannot afford to pay these people for their efforts right now, if you are familiar with the ways to get other people eager to work for you, you will have more talent than you really need. After all, investing a little time and talent is often more rewarding than investing in the stock market. When you invest in stock, you gamble. But when you get a person to invest his time and talent, he has the feeling that he is, in a way, controlling the results of the entire project. People feel that they are part of something when they help.

In any neighborhood, there has to be an accountant, a secretary, an advertising man, an office manager, a printer, a shipping man, and just about every other talent you might need for your Wealth-Building ideas. Who could resist the promise of future rewards for a little part-time help? Many people have added substantially to their income by offering such help to fledgling companies. Two teachers, one a teacher of commercial subjects and the other a manual arts instructor, gained a considerable interest in very successful businesses all because they were willing to spend a few hours a week helping a man long on ideas, but short on the experience these people had.

In fact, one man, Robert W., successfully assembled a group of people with the skills he needed by running a few classified ads in a local newspaper.

All he did was tell the truth. He stated that he was starting a business and needed help for which he could not pay—immediately. Not surprisingly, he was swamped with offers from people with every skill he needed. In fact, he even got the offer of additional seed capital from people who admired his very original approach. The people who did help him in his venture were ultimately given stock in his company, which is doing very well now, and is paying nice annual dividends to these far-sighted helpers.

USING ALL SOURCES OF O.P.T. TO BUILD WEALTH

How well do you really know your friends? Do you really know what they can do, other than what you have actually seen? For example, have you ever wondered what your co-workers might be able to do, other than the work for which they are now being paid?

You will be surprised at the amount of talent that lies below the surface of these people whom you thought you really knew all along. Frank S. made his living as an engineer for many years. But, in his spare moments, he had dabbled with a simple silk screen printing press. He never told anyone about his interests and talents. But, one day, a friend of his, Harry G., mentioned that he had an idea for some decorative wall hangings that could be produced by silk screen. Frank then told Harry about his press and his own interest in silk-screening and a very successful business venture was born immediately.

You don't even have to dig below the surface. Suppose that you are planning a home mail order business, but need help writing the sales messages. Perhaps the company you presently work for has an advertising manager who would welcome the opportunity to "moonlight" for you, writing the ads. Further, you might even be able to get professional help on the best way to handle the mailings and the shipping of the products from the shipping foreman of your company. Even the company bookkeeper might be interested in a part-time job for a piece of the action when the money starts to pour in.

Any social group, whether it is a lodge, church, profession, or trade club has many members who are often willing to donate their time and talent to help a friend get a business started. Don't be shy about asking. After all, it is the person with the positive mental attitude who attracts the help he needs. People like to be associated with a winner, and this attitude tells them that you will be a winner, and that they might be able to share in your future success.

HOW YOU CAN HAVE A MILLION DOLLAR SALES FORCE FOR NO SALARY AT ALL

For the part-time business operator, unless he is in the mail order business, selling is usually the most difficult of the problems. Here's how you can have a million dollar sales force without spending a penny in salaries.

The secret lies in using manufacturers' agents. These are independent businessmen who sell for several manufacturers at a time and work strictly for commissions on the sales they make. These men confine their sales activities to relatively narrow product lines. This means that they will be working quite hard for you. They strive to be very competent in their own area of specialization.

Here's how they will work for you. They solicit orders for you, and send the orders directly to you for shipment. You ship and bill the purchaser directly. Then, after you have been paid by the purchaser, you pay the commission to the agent. You retain all control over prices, terms, credit, and all the other conditions of sale. For this, however, most agents will expect that you give them exclusive rights to your products in their trading area. This is only fair, and doing so will make sure that your agents will work hard with your products.

Jeff D. is a manufacturers' agent in Florida, handling swimming pool equipment. Many of the companies Jeff represents are large and well-known, but he also handles quite a few small operations that make a good profit for him and the company owners.

Jeff's customers aren't the swimming pool owners, but rather the pool builders and those offering maintenance service for pool owners. Among the larger products handled by Jeff is a line of pumps and expensive filter systems. But, in addition to these products, he handles a line of specialty chemicals for pool cleaning and water treatment which are produced by a one-man garage operation.

Jeff works on an average of 35 percent mark-up on these lines and travels the entire state for the companies he represents. But, he is always on the lookout for more lines. After all, when he makes a call on a pool contractor, it's just as easy to show ten products as it is to show five. But, the products must be related so that he can sell them to his existing customers as he travels the state. Jeff does very well for himself—and for the manufacturers he represents.

Now, here is an even more important advantage of using an agent. Each and every one of them is a well-spring of information—all of it free. When they are trying to sell your products, the people they call on will ask them about other products. If they get enough of these questions, they will tell you and suggest ways of making the products and getting them to market. This is a million dollars worth of market research and it is absolutely free.

Using a manufacturers' agent will give you these important advantages:

Economy. It costs you nothing until a sale is made. You only pay a commission when the sale is made and the money has been collected from the customer. No high sales salary to worry about.

No run-away selling cost. Because you will pay a commission only when a sale is made, you will never be stuck with high selling costs when sales are down. As sales go up so do your commissions, but you will never mind paying these costs. As sales costs go down, so will your selling costs. This is what always chokes a big company with a large sales force. In a slump, they still have to continue to pay their salaried salesmen. But, you will only pay for orders delivered.

Intense sales coverage. Because most agents cover small segments of industry and geography, you will get intense coverage where you need it. You can pinpoint your important areas and get every cent of business from them.

Easy access to customers. Because most agents carry several other related, but noncompetitive lines, you will get immediate access to the customers you want. These men are already covering the area, and when they take on your line, you will automatically have coverage that takes years for an individual company salesman to get.

High quality salesmanship. More often than not, it is possible to get better sales coverage from an independent agent than from a salesman you might employ. Company salesmen, unless they are on a high commission basis, often become lazy when they reach a good income. However, the agent wants to keep your line, and will continue to sell hard for you.

Immediate sales. When you take on an agent who is already calling on the people you want to reach, you will have "instant sales." He doesn't have to spend his time developing the contacts. He already has them and it is simply a matter of introducing your products to the people he already numbers as his friends.

Automatic national sales offices. Once you have set up a network of agents across the country, you literally have a series of national sales offices. And, of course, this is a lot easier, and less expensive to administer than a network of your own salaried people in the same places.

Of course, there are disadvantages to using agents, but the advantages far outnumber them. There are two things to consider here. First, you seldom have any control over the way they sell. If you have developed any distinctive selling techniques, and your agent does not find them to his liking, he will not use them. But, as long as he gets the order, this can be a small matter. Second, because your agent will be carrying other lines, you will be getting only part-time coverage. But, remember that all of his lines must have something in common for him to make money. And, if he is calling on a company for one product, it is just as easy to pull yours out of the bag as well. In fact, it is for his benefit as well as yours.

HOW TO GET A NETWORK OF SALESMEN ... FREE

You can locate the manufacturers' agents you want in several ways. Here are some of the success-tested methods we have suggested to others:

- Advertise in the business pages of newspapers in the area where you seek sales.
- Advertise in the business publications that reach the motivated sales people you want. For example, for only a few dollars, you can reach well over 10,000 active agents

with a classified ad in *Agency Sales Magazine.* This is published by Manufacturers' Agents National Association, 3130 Wilshire Boulevard, Los Angeles, California 90010.

- Call the agents listed in the Yellow Pages of the phone book. You can go to the phone company's regional office and use their copies of out-of-town directories for reference.
- Get a copy of the *National Directory of Manufacturers Agents,* published by McGraw-Hill, 1221 Avenue of the Americas, New York, N.Y. 10020

SOLVING ALL OF YOUR EMPLOYMENT PROBLEMS . . . WITHOUT CHARGE

Even if you start out with one person to help you—and that person is a part-time employee—you will need some assistance in the personnel area. And, of course, as you grow, so will your needs for professional personnel help. You can get top help—without spending a nickel. Surely, you'd like to have someone:

- Determine the job requirements and locate the workers best qualified to do the work.
- Help you to keep the employees you have who are important to your growth.
- Plan personnel expansions and find the workers needed.
- Find and hire skilled workers in other parts of the country if there are none available in your area.
- Help you set up practical and easily-used personnel records and systems.
- Make use of free training programs for veterans.
- Help you to relocate your business in an area where

there is an ample supply of workers and desirable community facilities.

Yes, it is possible to have all these things—and more—done for you absolutely free. All you have to do is contact the local office of the United States Employment Service, describe your problems and requirements, and they will get the job done for you without charge. In fact, if you would like to know about all of the services you can tap free, write to the United States Employment Service, Bureau of Employment Security, U.S. Department of Labor, Washington, D.C. and ask for a copy of the publications of the U.S. Employment Service. This informative bulletin lists, describes, and explains how to order all Employment Service Bulletins which are available.

If you would like to receive monthly information on employment conditions in any state, simply write to the State Department of Labor in a particular state and ask them to put you on the list for their regular and free bulletins. There is a wealth of material in each of these monthly publications.

Remember this: when you use their services, you, and only you, are the final judge when it comes to hiring. But the Employment Service will pull out all the stops to find, test, and screen the people for you to make your personal choice. This is one of the best bargains available to the small businessman from the Federal Government. And, the price is right. It's free.

A MILLION DOLLARS WORTH OF FREE ADVERTISING CAN BE YOURS FOR THE ASKING

As mentioned earlier, it is possible to get the editors of most national magazines to run news releases and short articles on your new product or service by simply sending them a page of copy and a photo. This is part of their job, and they are always on the lookout for something new that will be of interest and benefit to their readers. But, suppose that you find it simply impossible to write this news release yourself and do not know where, or who, to send the releases to. The answer is simple. Use advertising O.P.T.

Ed C. had an idea for selling bird house kits by mail, but he was short on money. Ed thought that he might get the help of an advertising agency, but was staggered by the costs involved. However, the president of the agency thought that Ed had a good idea and he offered to do a news release and send it to all of the publications reaching people who would be interested in bird houses. The agency president did this without charge, but he did get Ed to agree to use his agency when and if the business became successful. About half a dozen magazines picked up the story and Ed was in business overnight. And, the agency president who had supplied the O.P.T. had acquired a client for life.

A well-planned and carefully written release can cost anywhere from $150 to $500. But, many an agency has found it to be quite profitable to do a release on "speculation" for a person who lacked money, but had good ideas. Be sure to look for a smaller agency to help you. The larger agencies are often overworked and are seldom interested in betting on the future of someone else's ideas.

Of course, when the release is prepared it will be sent to the editors of all the magazines that would be of value to you, and the editors then do their O.P.T. thing for you by running the item in their columns. The rest is up to you when the inquiries and orders flood you out of your basement workshop and send you rocketing up the ladder of business success.

HOW NEWSPAPER EDITORS CAN MAKE YOU RICH

If your business or service is to be offered strictly on a local basis, you can pull the same approach with a local newspaper editor. After all, he is interested in news, and a new business (which might become a future advertiser) is always welcomed for an editorial mention. As a matter of fact, you can use the approach described before with an advertising agency executive. He will, more than likely, be willing to lend a hand on a speculative basis. And, his connections with the local papers will be much stronger than yours are presently. Put the two together, and you have actually multiplied the power of Other People's Talent.

TAPPING THE O.P.T. OF EDUCATIONAL PROFESSIONALS

College and university professors are seldom overpaid. For this reason, many of them "moonlight" in their area of specialty. Most colleges have business departments, engineering departments, and other professionals available to lend an O.P.T. hand.

When Tom B. thought about starting a business of his own, he was immediately discouraged by both his lack of business experience and his limited funds. But, Tom was a good cook, and many people knew this. In fact, he used to "moonlight" from his drafting job to run cook-outs for local organizations. At one of his moonlighting cook-outs, Tom began chatting with a guest and told him of his one desire to do the thing he liked best—cooking.

It turned out that the man he was speaking with was a professor of business at a nearby college. The professor liked Tom—and his cooking—and offered to help him for a piece of the action, actually only 5 percent of the profits.

The professor, at his own expense, conducted a survey of the roads in town, and the eating habits of both the local residents and those just passing through. After spending considerable time, he was able to come up with a location and a restaurant idea that tapped both sources of customers. He was also able to use his business consulting influence to swing a loan with a local banker for the money needed to start the restaurant.

Within a very short time, Tom was in business, and the

professor not only had a percentage of the profits, he had also found a place to eat with a man who could outcook anyone else in town. Tom is now pocketing over $25,000 each year, and the professor has added about $1,200 a year to his income—for life.

You will be surprised how receptive these professionals will be to a well-conceived idea that can make money. Here are just some of the faculty people who can be of help and what they might be able to do for you:

Professors of accounting. They not only can help you to set up a bookkeeping system, they can counsel you on all the financial aspects of starting and running a business.

Marketing and advertising professors. They can guide you in your selling, advertising, and marketing.

Other business professors. You can get aid on personnel, administration, management, and just about every other aspect of business administration.

Professors of engineering. If you need help with product design or manufacture, these are the people to call on. One company developed a complete line of industrial products by using the chairman of the engineering department from a local college. They both profited very handsomely, but the company did not have the problem of paying a high-priced man during the stage when the products were being developed and there were no sales.

Psychologists. These men can be very helpful in handling personnel problems, as well as counseling on management and market research problems. Many can offer sound guidance on problems of consumer behavior which will relate to both product design and advertising.

Economists. Although economists tend to be more theoretical than other people, it is often possible to find one with his feet on the ground who can offer sound advice on short- and long-range business planning, as well as financial matters.

Special areas. If, for example, you are planning to do something in the art field, you can draw upon such talent in a college art department. The same for music. In fact, there is hardly an area of commerce where you will not be able to find a college faculty member with some expertise who would be willing to lend you his personal O.P.T.

HOW TO MAKE OTHER PROFESSIONAL PEOPLE— BANKERS, LAWYERS, AND ACCOUNTANTS— ANXIOUS TO FURTHER YOUR SUCCESS

Lawyers and accountants have two things to sell—time and talent. When you buy from them, they do not take a product off the shelf. They make their money giving you advice—advice that is based on many years of schooling and professional work. Therefore, when you seek the O.P.T. of these people, it is wise to approach them with this thought in mind. Here, you should emphasize that their help is actually an investment, much the same as it would be if they were to take thousands of dollars and place it in the stock market. But, you can play a trump card. When a man invests in the stock market, unless he is spending millions, he has absolutely no control over the company in which he is investing.

But, when he invests himself, by giving you the help you need, he will have a personal control over the possibility of future gain. The better he does his job of advising you, the better are his chances of making money when your enterprise makes it big.

For example, many lawyers have made fortunes, not in the courtrooms, but in the board rooms of the corporations they helped when they were just starting. The same holds true for accountants and even for bankers, where financial advice was the service offered.

When Ralph D., an attorney, was completing the work necessary to set up a corporation for Claude R., he found that

Claude had some very interesting ideas about how to make money servicing electronic equipment for local factories.

"How much money do you figure it would take to set up a business just to do this service work?" Ralph asked Claude at one of their meetings.

Claude's original purpose in setting up a company was to do TV service work, and he really hadn't thought much about how much money it would take to start this kind of business. But, he said, "$10,000 should be enough."

Before Claude left Ralph's office that day, the two had concluded a deal whereby Ralph would put up the $10,000 and throw in the legal services for only one third of the business. Now, instead of a simple TV repair business, Claude is in a big-time electronics repair business. His lawyer had sensed a way to make money, had given Claude the money and the legal help he needed, and a new business was born. Actually, Ralph had also gotten an accountant to do the books for only ten shares of corporate stock.

Last year, Claude had pocketed about $35,000, or about $15,000 more than he had expected to make when he sat down with Ralph to do the legal work on his original idea, a TV repair shop.

6

How to Control and Influence the People Who Can Help You Succeed

If there is one thing you will have to learn, it is the Wealth-Building Secret that people not only want to get along with other people, *they want to dominate them.* However, most people make the mistake of trying to gain power by using force. This will always fail. Only slaves or prisoners can be dominated by force, and they will rebel at the first opportunity. Power over people by force cannot be long maintained.

If you are going to make the most of the Wealth-Building Secrets in every chapter of this book, and you're going to influence and control people, you will have to learn to use more sophisticated methods than force. To see how these subtle, yet powerful methods can be used, read this story of Dave Andrews.

From James K. Van Fleet, *Miracle People Power* (West Nyack, N.Y., Parker Publishing Company, Inc., 1975)

HOW TO USE A PERSON'S MOST VULNERABLE POINT TO YOUR OWN ADVANTAGE

"A few years ago, I decided to sell our house in Springfield so I could buy one out in the country," Dave Andrews said. "I called the Landmark Real Estate Company and they sent a salesman, Bill Evans, out to see me. We talked for a while. Or I should say that I talked. Actually, Bill asked questions and I answered them.

"'You have a beautiful home here, Dave,' he said. 'Good part of town, excellent location, conveniently close to a new shopping center. Why on earth do you want to sell it and buy another house?

"'Is it too small for your needs? I understood you to say all your children were grown and gone. Or is it too large for you now? Does the room arrangement or space utilization dissatisfy you? Why don't you like your house, Dave? Tell me what's wrong with it so I'll be better able to know exactly how I can help you.'

"'Bill, I'll tell you the straight truth,' I said. 'There's absolutely nothing wrong with our house. I like it a great deal. If I could just pick it up and move it somewhere else, I'd keep it.

"'You see, when we first moved here, we had a beautiful view of the valley out the front room window: green fields and trees. Now all I can see is that new two-story house across the street. And the same thing is true in my back yard. All I can look at are my neighbor's garbage cans, his doghouse, the tool storage shed, and a barbecue pit. I want a home with a decent view I can enjoy.'

"'Good. Now I know exactly what you want and I have just the place you're looking for, Dave,' Bill said. 'Twenty miles out south of town. A beautiful home built on top of a hill. You can see for miles around. It has a gorgeous breath-taking overlook of the James River valley from the front porch. Nothing but green trees and miles of rolling pasture land. You'll love it, Dave. It's just what you're looking for.'

"So we drove out to see the place. Bill was right. It was everything I wanted. But the price was high. 'You're asking too much, Bill,' I said. 'My house is a newer one and you know I can't begin to get that kind of a price for it.'

"Bill didn't argue. 'Could be, Dave,' he said. 'But just look at that view of the lake. No one'll ever be able to build anything that will keep you from seeing it. That view belongs to you from now on. No one will ever be able to take it away from you.'

"'But I don't think I can afford it, Bill,' I said. 'I don't have that kind of money lying around loose, and besides . . .'

"'Financing is no problem, Dave,' Bill said, interrupting me. 'I know of no less than five lending institutions who would lend you the money today without a single question. Your credit rating is tops. I checked that before I ever left the office.

"'And just look at that view from the front room window here, Dave. Isn't that absolutely spectacular? No house across the street to block your view of the beautiful James River valley. And there never will be. The way the hill drops off, you don't need to worry about anyone ever building on it. This is exactly what you asked for, Dave. This is precisely what you said you wanted.'

"Each time I talked price or money or financing, Bill talked scenery and a beautiful view of the lake and the James River valley, for he knew full well that's what I was primarily interested in. I'd already told him that back at my house. By asking questions and by listening to my answers, Bill had found my main point of interest. He'd found my most vulnerable point and he concentrated on that.

"So I bought the house. Or I should say I bought the view, for that's what Bill actually sold me. He sold me the view and the scenery . . . the lake and the trees . . . the James River valley and its rolling pasture land. He just threw in the house as an extra bonus; it was an additional dividend.

"Now I'd never met Bill Evans before that day. He and I were complete strangers until I bought that house. But just as soon as Bill found out exactly what I wanted and then showed me how to get it, he took charge of the situation. He held me in the palm of his hand for he was in complete control."

You can use the same techniques Bill Evans used with Dave Andrews to get what you want, too. When you find out precisely what a person wants and then show him how to get it, when you discover a man's most vulnerable point and then concentrate on that, and on that alone, you'll be able to influence and control everyone you meet, too, whether they're strangers or not. In fact, when you do that. . .

YOU'LL GAIN THESE BENEFITS

How you'll be able to influence the thoughts and actions of a total stranger

The moment you find out exactly what a person wants and then show him how to get it, you'll be in complete command of the situation the same way Bill Evans was. You'll be able to influence the thoughts and ideas of a complete stranger. You'll have the ability to control the decisions and actions of a person you've never met before when you show him precisely how to get what he wants.

How controlling his decisions will help you

When you can influence and control another person's thoughts and actions, when you show him how he'll get what he wants if he does as you want him to do, you'll make more money and gain more of the material benefits of life for yourself. You can't help but become successful, for finding out what a person wants and showing him how to get it are the most important Wealth-Building Secrets in this book.

Knowledge that means unlimited power for you

When you know what another person really wants and then show him how to get it, you'll have a miracle people power in your grasp that few persons understand and even fewer ever possess.

If you know everything there is to know about a person, you can use that knowledge for your own benefit and to your own advantage. When you know what your husband wants, what your boss is thinking, what your competitor is doing, what your girl friend has on her mind, what the teacher is planning— you're truly in a most enviable position.

Finding out specifically what people want and then helping them get it is not only the most important secret of business and salesmanship, but it is also the number one rule in all your relationships with other people. It is a real key to miracle people power and a definite sound philosophy to practice and live by.

TECHNIQUES YOU CAN USE TO GAIN THE BENEFITS

The formula to power, influence, and control over other people is broken down into three simple techniques:

1. Know how you can fulfill one or more of a person's innermost needs and desires.
2. Find out *specifically* what a person wants.
3. Help him get what he wants.

When you look over these three techniques, you can see how Bill Evans used them. First of all, Bill knew what he had to offer. He knew how he could fulfill a person's innermost needs and desires. Second, he found out specifically what Dave was looking for. Third, Bill showed Dave exactly how he could get what he wanted.

Now let's look at those three techniques in even more detail so you can see how you can make them work for you, too.

Knowing how you can fulfill one or more of a person's innermost needs and desires

This technique requires two things of you. The first requirement is that you know and understand and appreciate the average normal person's innermost needs and desires. The second one is that you must know exactly how your product or your service or how you yourself can fulfill that person's basic needs and desires.

You already know what those innermost needs and desires are. Now you need to analyze your own product, service, or proposition to find out exactly how you can help your listener and which of his basic needs and desires you can fulfill. To do this, you need knowledge about what you have to offer. You must know exactly how you can help a person and what you can do for him.

Bill Evans knew how to do that when he sold Dave a house. He didn't just sell a house. He offered Dave liberty from the restrictions and crowded conditions of city living. He gave him the chance to escape from the congestion, the pollution, and the noise of traffic. He offered Dave the opportunity to live as he wanted to live and to enjoy the unspoiled beauty of nature. Dave also gained a sense of personal power over his environment when he knew no one would ever to be able to spoil his view of the lake and the James River valley.

When Dave was able to fulfill these basic needs, he was also able to gain emotional security, for emotional security cannot be achieved unless you are able to fulfill all your innermost desires.

A good way to learn how big companies and corporations slant their advertising toward the fulfillment of your innermost needs and desires is to analyze their TV commercials and study their newspaper and magazine advertisements. It's a lot of fun and highly informative. You can learn a lot by watching how the professionals do it.

Finding out *specifically* what a person wants

After you know exactly what you have to offer, your next step is to find out *specifically* what a person wants. It is important to note that *whatever a person is lacking at the moment he has the greatest need and desire for.* And that's your job: to discover his greatest need and desire; to find out exactly what he wants.

And what's the best way to find out? That's right; by asking questions. Asking questions is still the most reliable and fastest way to find out precisely what your listener wants.

You can get specific answers to your questions when you use the question words *who, what, when, where, why, how,* and *how much.* Here are some of the benefits you can gain by asking questions and using those simple question words.

Questions help your listener concentrate his attention. By asking questions you can help a person focus his attention where you want it. He literally sells himself on your idea and then talks himself into believing it was his own idea in the first place. When you ask questions, you help a person make up his mind about what he actually wants.

"I've found the lecture method to be the poorest way to teach," says Joyce Hopkins, a high school history teacher. "When I ask questions and give my students the chance to answer them fully, it helps them concentrate their attention on the subject matter at hand. Their minds don't wander away; they stay more alert. Not only that, questions stimulate full group participation and discussion."

Questions make a person feel important. When you ask a person for his opinion or his idea on anything, you make him feel more important. This in itself fulfills one of his innermost needs and desires. When you show him that you respect his opinion on the subject, he'll be more likely to respect yours and do as you want him to do.

"Want to have a happy marriage?" says Dr. Gerald Beasley. "Then pay attention to your partner; make your spouse important. How? One of the easiest ways I know is to ask questions. Just be sure they're the right kind of questions—ones that are designed to make the person feel important, needed, and useful.

"For instance, if you're the wife, ask him questions to get him to talk about himself, his work, and so on. And if you're the husband, do the same thing. A wife often feels left out of major decisions. Ask for her opinion. Let her know that you value and respect her judgment."

You'll keep from talking too much. Often, people lose arguments and salesmen lose sales because they talk when they should be listening. When you ask questions, the other person has the chance to tell you what he thinks and what he wants. All you need do is keep quiet and give him the opportunity to talk.

Raymond Campbell is in charge of industrial relations for the Mono Manufacturing Company in Joplin, Missouri. "Most people think my job is solving employee problems or settling labor grievances," Ray says. "Actually, I let people solve their own problems by talking them out with me. I just act as a sounding board for their frustrations. I ask a few questions here and there to stimulate their thinking. Then I sit back and listen. Keeps me from talking too much and spoiling things."

You can avoid getting into an argument. By asking questions, you can find out what the other person's idea is first. If you tell him what you think, if you give him your opinion first, you expose your own position. You may suddenly find yourself at odds with him and lose all possibilities of getting your own way. If you don't agree with what he says, don't tell him so point-blank. Use Jerry Dunlap's method.

"I don't tell a person straight out I don't agree with him," Jerry says. "Instead, I say, *'Don't you think* it might be better this way, George?' *'Don't you feel* this would save you more time, Anna?' *'Doesn't this seem* like a good way to do it, Mary?'

"This way I'm telling a person in a courteous way what I think and I'm asking him at the same time to respond with his opinion or idea. It gets much better results than saying, 'Do it this way, period!'"

When you ask questions, you can find out specifically what a person wants. A question is still the quickest way to find out what another person really wants. Questions help you find the key issue, a person's most vulnerable point, his major weakness, his greatest desire.

When you do discover his main point of interest or his most important need—concentrate on that and on that alone. Don't ramble around aimlessly from point to point scattering your fire. You can use this one key issue to get your own way.

Helping him get what he wants

After you find out specifically what a person wants, then you must help him get it. Take Bill Evans again, for instance. Just to find out what Dave wanted was not enough. Bill had to help Dave get what he wanted the easiest way possible.

Bill did this by finding out that Dave's credit rating was okay . . . that several lending institutions would lend him the money . . . by showing him that he really could afford to buy the house. Bill did everything he could to help Dave get what he wanted. And he did it in such a way that Dave had no choice but to say yes. That's what you must do for your listener, too.

Here's another example to show you how this technique will work in every kind of situation.

"A few years ago when I was a general foreman for the St. Louis plant, one of our Canadian plants ran into all sorts of production problems," Hugh Curtis says. "The vice president in charge of manufacturing up in Dayton told our plant manager,

Glen Dawson, to transfer someone up there to straighten things out. Glen told our production superintendent, Joe Freeman, that he could go or that he could send me. Well, Joe picked me to go.

"It couldn't have been a worse time for me to move. My youngest son was graduating from college; my wife had just come home from the hospital; my oldest daughter's baby was due in June; we were right in the middle of building a new house.

"I wanted to stay where I was in the worst way, but I didn't want to give Joe a lot of excuses for not wanting the transfer either. I gave a lot of thought about how to handle it. Here's what I finally told him:

"'Joe, you know I'm really honored by your picking me to go up to Canada to help them out,' I said, 'but I just wonder how they'll react to a general foreman telling a plant manager where he's wrong.

"'Now if you were to go, there'd be no problem like that. After all, you're the production superintendent here and you act in the plant manager's place when Glen is gone. They'd listen to you.

"'Not only that, it would really make you look good up in Dayton when you straighten up their mess. I really think an important job like that needs a big man like you with your experience and know-how to solve their problems, Joe.'

"Well, Joe took the job. You see, I was able to show him how he could fulfill several of his basic needs and desires by taking this transfer. Specifically he acquired: a feeling of importance; recognition of efforts; a sense of personal power; further financial success in the form of a promotion. These were Joe's most vulnerable points.

"But if I'd approached Joe with all the reasons why I didn't want to go, I'd be there and he'd still be here."

Now at first glance, you might think that to use a person's most vulnerable points to your own advantage has a sinister sound to it. Nothing of the sort. There's nothing evil about the idea at all. You're actually using a person's most vulnerable points to help him get what he wants.

You see, the only way you can ever find out what a person really wants is to discover the main issue—this will be his most vulnerable point—and then concentrate on that and on that alone.

Only then will you be able to help a person by showing him how to get what he really wants. And when you help another person get what he wants, you automatically get what you want, too.

Sometimes a person isn't really sure of what he wants most. He has to be shown what he wants just as Hugh Curtis showed Joe Freeman. So if a person isn't sure, help him find out. That's part of your job, too.

7

How to Use Big-Time Advertising Secrets to Make Your Business Grow

If you intend to make big money in your spare time, then you must learn to promote what you do. With a little ingenuity on your part, however, you can get results that will literally amaze you.

Some time ago, Bob Beacher, a Salt Lake City retail store clerk trying to raise a family of four on less than $4500 a year, invented a new whip-top toy that delighted children and looked as though it would sell well provided he could let the public know about it.

Using his imagination, Bob sat down at his kitchen table for 30 minutes a day and, utilizing the methods outlined in this chapter, began to promote his product. The results: Thousands of dollars worth of whip-tops sold, publicity that spanned the nation and a growing business that eventually topped $300,000 a year.

From Duane G. Newcomb, *Spare-Time Fortune Guide* (West Nyack, N.Y., Parker Publishing Company, Inc., 1973)

HOW TO MAKE AND USE NEWS
RELEASES EFFECTIVELY

In the first place, you will want to use two kinds of releases—newspaper and magazine. If you're selling a product, a
magazine news release will be quite effective. See Figure 7-A for
the style to use when preparing a New Product Release.

THROWABLE LIFE PRESERVER
IS SELF-INFLATING

The odds favoring successful rescue of a drowning
person are greatly improved by this new SAV-A-LIFE
Rescue Ball, because it can be thrown with accuracy
much farther and far *more* accurately than conventional life preservers.

SAV-A-LIFE was designed to fill a gap in water rescue and water safety which has long been neglected
and impractical for most present life saving devices.

Most people can't throw a life jacket or ordinary life-
ring more than 20 or 30 feet, and it takes practice to
place it with any accuracy. SAV-A-LIFE, about the
size and shape of an indoor baseball, has good throw-
ing weight of 9½ ounces, and can easily be thrown
with accuracy up to 200 feet to cover 40 times the
effective rescue area.

The unit is activated by the water entering the ball
through openings, and within seconds after it hits the
water the ball opens and out springs a full-size self-
inflating life preserver with enough buoyancy to support a 250 lb. person. At the same time a small

---

anchor is dropped to keep the life preserver from drifting out of reach. It is also "Rechargeable" for re-use.

The small compact size of SAV-A-LIFE makes it easy to carry or store in a boat, tackle box, beach bag, car glove compartment—trunk or many other places where other life preservers can't. Even fits most pockets, allowing those who work or play near water to have constant access to this "baseball-size" Life-Saving Device.

SAV-A-LIFE, priced at $5.95, is manufactured by INVENTORS PRODUCTS COMPANY, 4309 Edina Industrial Blvd., Minneapolis, Minnesota 55435.

FIGURE 7-A. NEW PRODUCT RELEASE—This kind is extremely effective for introducing new products.

In addition, newspaper releases are effective for announcing activities you're handling or projects you're going into. Since your local newspaper often will pick up what you're doing, contact the editor with a news release any time you open business, add some employees, start a new project, or anything similar.

Bill Borden, for instance, opened a new janitorial service in a small town and solicited five of the local churches as his first clients.

He then wrote up what he was going to do and sent this to the newspaper, along with a picture. The results—excellent exposure.

The rules are:

1. State "For Immediate Release" in the upper left hand corner.

2. Put the date in the upper right hand corner.

3. Give the release a title. In this case, "Local Boy Opens New Service."
4. Tell what you're doing, list the people you're working with, and anything else that might prove interesting (see Figure 7-B).

IS IT A BIRD? IS IT A PLANE? IS IT SUPERMAN? NO, IT'S A DELTA WING, THE HOT NEW ITEM IN WATER SKIING

The hottest new twist to water skiing is an idea put forth by Leonardo da Vinci about 500 years ago—the concept of "wings-for-man." This now takes form in the dart-shaped, delta wing kite which is breaking all records for air-borne skiers.

Standard kites have been flown in this country nearly 20 years. However, the delta wing is a recent import from Australia where, for the past two years, the Aussies have been soaring at heights usually reserved for aircraft.

The basic difference between the standard, rigid kite and the delta wing is this: A skier with a standard kite is entirely dependent upon boat driver and boat speed for his altitude; that is, he ascends and descends in relation to the speed of his tow boat and his tow line remains attached to the boat at all times.

The delta wing skier is his own "pilot." He can control his rise and descent with a base bar which is comparable to a "joy stick" in early aircraft. He can also cut himself loose, at will, for a free fall. In this maneuver he is much like a glider pilot, soaring on the wings of the wind.

"There's a world of difference between the two types of kites," according to 30-year-old Richard Johnson, Winter Haven, Fla. "With the delta wing, you're in complete control of your altitude. Once you cut loose, you can pinpoint your landing."

Johnson is a water ski instructor at his own ski school in Winter Haven. Among his former students is astronaut Allen B. Shepperd. Johnson appears as a ski coach in a new motion picture produced by Evinrude Motors for release next spring.

FIGURE 7-B. A NEWSPAPER RELEASE—This kind can be made up for many different types of activities.

Using Borden's example, you can make up your own.

If you live in a community with throw-away shoppers' newspapers and a number of overlapping local newspapers, by all means send your release to the editor of every possible paper. Include your name and address so he can get back to you if there are questions.

HOW TO MAKE THE LOCAL PRESS PAY OFF

In order to really make your activities hop, you must become known locally. To do this, you should frequently have items in your local paper. Doing this effectively requires a system. The paper won't print your name just because you want it to, but it will print it if you're doing something that creates news. In short, you have to use your imagination and invent things to do that the newspapers will want to print.

Now, here are a few rules:

1. Do something unusual on special occasions.

2. Make a splash at holiday time.

3. Do something different that's appropriate with the season.

4. Dream up a special project or activity.

5. Do something for charity.

6. Do something unusual or special for the community.

Now let's see how one energetic young woman used this program:

Helen Hanson, a San Francisco divorcee who was having a hard time keeping her family clothed and fed on $200 a month, began a baby-sitting service about two years ago. This service did just moderately well until last fall, when she learned how to let the newspaper work for her. After that her business really took off.

At Christmas time, for instance, Helen got permission from the parents of the children she cared for to involve them in various worthy charitable projects. She then had her children make up baskets for the poor—the day before Christmas they delivered these baskets to the needy families in the neighborhood. Naturally, she let the newspapers know about it.

As summer approached, she held a special summer picnic for her children's families in the local park. This included a ceremony in which she gave the kids awards for little projects they had completed. Naturally, she took pictures and sent them to the local paper, along with the names of the kids who won the awards.

Next, she held a "Help The Elderly" project—a clean-up of a widow's yard near her "school." This resulted in more publicity. The kids also participated in a march for the local heart fund, and took on a project to pick up papers and trash around their neighborhood. Each time they did something, Helen sent in a news release and a picture which resulted in extra publicity and brought all the business she could use. Today, this part-time "school" brings in roughly $13,000 a year.

HOW TO TURN TELEVISION AND
RADIO INTO A GOLD MINE

You, too, can appear on local television and radio. Many stations have interview shows that are constantly looking for guests. No matter what kind of activity you've decided to go into, there's something about it that the other people will be interested in hearing about.

Milton Thomas, for instance, a low-paid Miami hotel worker, needed extra money to pay for a number of department store bills his wife had run up, and decided to start a part-time small appliance fix-it service in his home.

There wasn't anything unusual about Milton's business, but he realized that people frequently got mad when they discovered that it was often cheaper to buy a whole new small appliance than to have it repaired. To get on local radio and TV shows, Milton simply called the local radio and TV stations and asked whom to contact. He then wrote each one a letter explaining he could talk about why there was a problem and what the individual homeowner could do about it. The results: He appeared on four radio stations and one TV station. The stations received several hundred calls and Milton's income jumped almost immediately from $100 a month extra to over $1,000. Milton not only paid off his wife's bills in short order, but also acquired a brand new car and a $40,000 home in a nearby suburban community.

To do this yourself, pick out something you do that has universal appeal. If you started a small mail order business, you might want to stress the fact that many people today are interested in mail order, plus the ins and outs of getting started; if it's a lawn and garden service, you might talk about how home-owners should care for their lawns; if it's a re-mailing service, you might stress that hundreds of people need someone to re-mail their personal mail for them, and go into the reasons why.

Simply pick out that topic that has good general interest.

Either call or write the station directly. It's best to call first and get the names of the people you should contact. Here's a sample letter to help you get started (see Figure 7-C).

> Belt T. Thomas
> 888 Bilton St.
> Round About, N.H.

Mr. Thomas Gibbs
Talk Around
KLTV
808 7th St.
Round About, N.H.

Dear Mr. Gibbs:

Did you know that hundreds of people have a large num-ber of their letters re-mailed from an address miles away from their home state?

No? I'll bet your listeners didn't either. Many mailers don't want their ex-wives to know where they are—others are dodging creditors, and some are hiding out from relatives—be-sides this, of course, there are a thousand other reasons.

Having been in the re-mailing business for three years, I can discuss the reasons why people re-mail and cite hundreds of interesting examples.

I'm sure this would make an interesting discussion show for your listeners—if you'd like to have me come on, call me at 922-4312.

> Sincerely,
>
> _____
>
> Belt T. Thomas

FIGURE 7-C

HOW TO CREATE A SPLASH
BOTH LOCALLY AND NATIONALLY

This isn't easy, but you can do it. The secret simply is to keep up a news release barrage to both newspapers and magazines. You must, however, be selective.

First, take your project and list ten things about it that are unique or unusual. For instance, one retiree raising earthworms, 69-year-old Leo Banmore, listed these facts:

1. Starting with 20,000 worms, you will have two million in one year.

2. Earthworms double every two months.

3. Eggs are contained in the ring around the neck.

4. Earthworms can be grown in peat moss, corn meal, ground walnut shells and other media.

5. Millions are sold each year to fishermen.

6. The castings from the earthworms make a good fertilizer that nurseries will buy.

7. One man has recently come up with a method to make earthworms edible.

8. Over ten thousand people raise earthworms in the U.S.

9. Some women sell over a million a year.

10. You can raise over two million earthworms in about fifty feet of space.

With this list in mind, he watches the newspaper and tries to tie into community events.

The trick, he finds, is to be creative. For instance:

1. Just before fishing season, he takes a picture of a pretty girl digging up some worms on his "farm" and sends it to the

local newspaper, with the caption: "Fishing Time Again—Pretty Anita Coleman gets set to dig up some fishing worms for the season's opener at Banmore's Worm Farm in Sacramento. On Saturday, over 50,000 local residents are expected to head for the woods and streams, many of them fishing with worms from farms like Banmore's."

2. During Easter vacation, he hired a half dozen college students and sent a news release to both newspapers and magazines, stressing the unusual occupations that youths can sometimes get into on part-time jobs. The result—eight newspaper and two magazine pick-ups.

3. He wrote a short release on how to raise worms as a part-time business and sent it to 200 magazines and newspapers—this brought stories in eight newspapers and four magazines. This technique, of course, requires imagination. It isn't easy, but it can be done. Try to decide what things people would be interested in (as far as your project is concerned), tie it together with some newsworthy event and make up a release.

PROMOTE YOURSELF WITH THE PEOPLE WHO REALLY COUNT

One rule that the experts in this business constantly stress: Don't promote indiscriminately, but try to "rifle" your approach. (You'll probably want to disregard this when sending out news releases, but nowhere else.) With direct mail, or any other kind of promotion, you must go directly to people who will buy.

To reach them effectively, you must first sit down and decide who your potential customers really are.

Let's take our worm farm. Banmore decided worms could be sold effectively to grocery stores, drug stores and automotive chains selling fishing tackle, plus sporting goods stores, resorts and more. He then made a list of the ten top grocery chains in the United States handling sporting goods, the 20 top sporting goods stores, large automotive chains with sporting goods departments (like Grand Auto in California and Oklahoma Tire & Supply, Tulsa, Oklahoma), and large resorts catering to fishermen. His list contained 200 names. He then sent a series of sales letters directly to the buyers at these firms. All this effort resulted in many sales.

The rules, then:

1. Decide who'll buy your product.
2. Select the top prospects.
3. Plan and launch your attack.

HOW TO USE THE PHONE EFFECTIVELY

Make no mistake about it, your phone is one of the best promotional tools you have. It costs no more to make it work for you than it does not to use it. In addition, it can probably bring you as much, or more, business than any other kind of promotional tool.

First, you must be systematic. Decide that you will call five prospects on a regular daily, weekly or monthly basis. In calling, be sure to do your homework. Sit down and make a list of people who could use your services or products. Decide what their needs are and how you can meet those needs. Then call and explain what you have in mind. You should, of course, always try to put an extra twist on your pitch—one that makes what you're offering especially useful to your prospect.

Now, let's see how this works:

Let's say you've developed a calculator for figuring the correct angle for such things as picture frames. You know this is an item that home craftsmen need. Since you're wholesaling this item, you decide companies selling power tools would be good prospects. These could be demonstrated in action with a power saw to produce traffic for higher ticket items.

On your list you'll include Sears, Montgomery Ward, local hardware stores selling craftsmen's tools, chains specializing in do-it-yourself for home owners, lumber yards with a power tool line, and more.

Next, say that you've noticed in the paper that a local chain specializing in home do-it-yourself items is running a power tool sale. You reason they could very well use somebody giving an actual demonstration of your item to create traffic. In contacting them, call the president or general manager—tell him what you want and ask if he can put you in touch with the person responsible for this promotion.

Second, you explain that this is a traffic-building opportunity for them—that you will come in and put on the demonstration and that demonstrations like this, with all the noise and uproar, ordinarily attract attention and pull crowds.

You may not get to do it, but you have started learning to use your telephone as a promotional tool. Now keep at it—keeping the needs of your prospect in mind. Again, go to the top person first, and let him direct you to whoever can help.

Now, let's take an example on a smaller scale.

You have started a small part-time janitorial service, and you want to line up prospects. As you drive around, note the buildings going up that might be prospects for your services. In your calls, call the construction company putting up the building, ask them who's going to be responsible for its management—call them and tell them what you can do.

Again, remember their needs. If the new building has lots of glass, stress your window washing capabilities. If they're installing a special type of flooring, stress your ability to handle this. In other words, find out what they need and try to fill it.

Besides calling five new prospects regularly, you should also use the phone several other ways.

Keep the list of names and phone numbers of anyone who contacts you about business. Make up a card file of these names and regularly check back with them to see if they've obtained this service somewhere else, or if they're ready to use yours.

Let's say you're acting as a sales outlet for a particular kind of air conditioning. Over the weeks a number of people have expressed an interest in your product. What you must do is to call them back regularly, say every three or four months, and ask them if they're ready to buy now. Since you've talked to them once before, always remind them who you are, then tell them what you have to offer. The rule is always to offer something extra on each call. For instance, you can call if you have a new model—if there's a special price on some models, or something has come up you thought they would be interested in. You must, however, always include this kind of extra appeal.

People using this type of telephone promotion find they're making sales or selling their services a year after the first contact. In addition, after a period of time they're producing a steady stream of sales.

In addition to this kind of telephone activity, you can also promote with incoming calls.

A cardinal rule here is that you must always see people in person to convert telephone calls into actual sales. This is an art that requires much practice. For instance, a call comes in and somebody inquires about your prices for a lawn-keeping service. You don't simply give them the price, you say: "We try to keep our prices extremely reasonable—it's probably below most others. However, there isn't any way I can give you a firm price until I can see your yard. If you like, I can come over and give you an estimate today."

You now have your foot in the door, and a chance of doing some real business.

Let's take another example—suppose you're running a small fix-it shop. You say: "A lot of times I can fix it for a very reasonable fee, but the only way I can really tell is to see your item. Why don't you come in and let me give you an accurate estimate."

The rule: Always either ask them to come in so you can

give them a firm price, or offer to go out and give them an estimate in person. This way, you convert people at the other end of the phone into actual prospects.

HOW TO GET OTHERS
TO SELL FOR YOU

Other people can really help sell for you. The trick is to know how to get them to do it.

To get people to talk about what you're doing, you, yourself, must talk about it. Whenever you get a chance, talk about your activities—show enthusiasm, and let people know it's the greatest thing you've ever done. That's all there is to it.

If you're extremely enthusiastic, people you talk to will talk to others about you—although this seems too simple a method to really work, don't underestimate it, for it will carry your name and activities further than you ever dreamed possible.

8

How to Use the Selling Secrets of the Professionals to Build a Fortune

"Nothing happens until somebody sells something," a quote from Arthur H. Motley, publisher of *Parade* magazine, highlights why salesmen earn high pay. Sales are the key to profits—so anyone who can really "move the goods" earns a healthy slice of the income produced. Check these points—

Sales incomes increased more during a recent three-year period than any other group's income. Figures compiled by the Research Institute of America, Inc. show salesmen's pay climbed 18 percent, executive compensation 17 percent, middle-management and professionals (doctors, lawyers, and dentists) 14 percent, and clerical and production workers 12 percent. During the same period, the cost of living as measured by the Consumers Price Index rose 8.6 percent.

From Merle E. Dowd, *How to Earn a Fortune and Become Independent in Your Own Business* (West Nyack, N.Y., Parker Publishing Company, Inc., 1971)

Presidents of 27 percent of America's corporations scrambled to their pinnacle through sales and marketing, according to a survey by the Council on Opportunities in Selling, Inc.

During the first year following a switch from some other occupation, salesmen finishing a professional sales training course averaged a 34 percent increase in income—with some incomes up as much as 300 percent.

Salesmen ranked second in the list of average incomes—entertainers captured the top spot at $25,000 plus per year. Salesmen were next at $20,000-$22,000, followed closely by the medical and law professionals at $18,000-$20,000. When these figures were compiled, only 2 percent of the working population earned $19,000 per year or more.

Producing salesmen frequently earn more than the president. In one Ohio manufacturing company, two salesmen earn more than the president—however, he's glad to pay them because their sales keep the company alive and prospering.

Examples of men and women who doubled or tripled their incomes by switching into sales come more easily than for any other profession. Take the case of Don Elmers, former Director of Music Education in a fashionable suburban junior and high school system. Don inspired students to plug away at their band instruments, beginning in the fifth grade. He and his associate director turned out one prize-winning group after another. But, Don was caught in a salary schedule fixed by his graduate degree and years of experience. He couldn't earn another nickel despite how good he might be as a teacher. At age 30, the road ahead looked bleak with only a minimum increase in salary programmed, a schedule that always seemed to lag behind yearly increases in the cost of living.

To break out of the trap, Don registered in the Sales Training, Inc. (STI) program called "Whole Man Development." For six months he studied on his own in the evening while continuing to work days at the school. After spring classes closed, he attended STI full time to graduate as an honor student. Immediately he went into insurance sales. The high school lost a talented and inspiring music teacher—but Penn-Mutual Insurance gained a highly motivated, professionally trained salesman. Within three months, Don was selling at the rate of $1,200,000 of insurance per year plus occasional special-purpose coverages he arranged as a broker to meet unusual requirements. One month out of three he topped applications and sales for the local office. His estimated increase in income—about 150 percent. How did he do it? Several factors are important—

Don radiates enthusiasm. He transferred the same kind of infectious spirit that motivated kids to practice their horns into sales presentations for a product he believed in—whole life insurance.

He words hard, scheduling meetings with prospects as early as 7 in the morning for breakfast to as late as 8:30 in the evening. During the middle of the day, he processes the never ending piles of paper. Does he mind the long hours? Not at all—because he is excited about his job—and his excitement shows and pays off.

Professional training in sales techniques, confidence, and motivation building, plus a continually increasing knowledge of the immensely complex insurance business contribute to Don's sales ability.

Is Don happy about changing from his first love of music and teaching to selling insurance? "Of course I liked teaching music. That's why I spent so many years in college. But, now I have to pinch myself every morning just to make sure I'm not dreaming. Changing to sales was the greatest thing that ever happened to me."

CHANGING TO SALES

Change appears to be the order of the day for many successful transplants from dead-end jobs, income-limited jobs, military careers, and from one kind of selling to another. Just a few examples—

Harry K—trained himself intensively for law enforcement work and worked for the Denver county sheriff's office, but, in time, he found that looking at the wrong end of a gun could be disquieting and not financially rewarding. So, he began servicing dictation equipment, utilizing his Army electronic training in radio, radar, and electronics. The job of servicing equipment also promised limited long-term potential. So Harry, never one to give up easily, started once again, this time in sales. While continuing to work at service and repair, Harry enrolled in Sales Training. He earned the first vacancy in the dictation firm's sales staff. Immediately his volume of sales took off. He knew the equipment from the inside out. During the first full year after completing his training, sales volume expanded and his income tripled over his earnings as a service representative.

Stephen W—found himself with a severance paycheck and no job shortly after passing his 50th birthday, a casualty of a merger. Although he had spent 25 years with his company, the shakeout of middle and near-top management personnel when the new top brass took over found him in that all-too-familiar position—too old to find a new job in planning and budgeting and too young to retire. Discouraged after more than three months of looking for another management position, he decided to make a fresh start. "Nobody in personnel can tell you outright that you're too old for a job they have in mind," Stephen reported. "That would be illegal, discrimination due to age. But, you get the message after being turned down again and again." With his usual analytic approach, Stephen examined every likely possibility. He didn't have years to build up a new reputation. He was a man in a hurry to begin earning his $25,000-plus salary again. At the end of every road he looked at, the same sign loomed—SALES. He made another wise choice and sought out a complete, professional training program for sales. By attending classes full time, he finished a complete sales training course in half the normal time. Job opportunities immediately opened. He started selling office supplies full time. In less than one year his net earnings topped the $25,000 annual rate he had spent 25 years attaining—with no ceiling in sight.

William R—faced another kind of problem. He retired from the Army with the rank of Major after 22 years of service but with no professional or vocational training. His boys were in junior high school. College expenses loomed over the near horizon. Retirement pay without the allowances he had learned to live with wouldn't meet his desired standard of living. So, Bill took his disciplined mind into sales. His mature approach and military bearing helped him to sell mutual fund shares for a local brokerage firm. But, too many prospects failed to buy, and he was about to lose out when an associate suggested he learn more about the psychology and mechanics of selling. Training followed, and even before he was through with his training his volume doubled—and he is still completing sales at an ever increasing clip.

With so many opportunities—really good opportunities for increasing income—available, why are so many lucrative sales jobs going begging? Probably the answer lies in the image conjured up in people's minds when they hear "salesman" or "selling." Try it yourself—what pops into your mind first when you hear the term salesman? Do you think of the door-to-door type who knocks at your front door with a case of pots and pans? Or the "student working his way through college?" The high-pressure used-car pusher and fast closer who confuses more than helps? Possibly the sales agent for a here-today-gone-tomorrow home improvement contractor with his "special deal?"

Dramatists have done little to brighten the image of selling as a profession. *Death of a Salesman* with its highly dramatic message and caricature of the back-slapping, man-to-man salesman probably set back the profession of selling more than any one example of negative image building—despite the play's dramatic success. Harold Hill in the *Music Man* similarly characterized the "drummer" image associated with selling. Despite the picture of selling instilled in many minds, a salesman's status and how people feel about his job may affect your decision to change. The image and the salesman's performance and self-satisfaction are improving. For example:

A President of the United States has said: "The salesman is a key figure in an economy which relies upon individual initiative and the competitive forces of the marketplace to stimulate full employment and achieve an orderly and efficient distribution of our goods and services. Our salesmen and saleswomen are the creative organizers of the free market so vital to the growth, prosperity, and well-being of our nation."

Answers from a survey of nearly 1,000 of the biggest corporations in the U.S., as reported in *The Salesman—Ambassador of Progress,* a publication of the Sales and Marketing Executives-International, clearly note the increasing status of salesmen—

> "Salesmen are becoming more important in our business"—79 percent.

> "We are employing more salesmen than we did five years ago"—74 percent.

> "Business profits do not come from making things—profits come from *selling* the things that business makes"—92 percent.

> "No, we do not think salesmen suffer from a low social status"—92 percent.

> "Absolutely not!" 92 percent of the chief executives replied in answer to the question—"Do you think that salesmen have questionable ethics?"

> "Would you, as sales managers, counsel your sons to go into selling?" Answer—96 percent—"Yes!"

> Wives answered—"My husband travels a lot, of course, but our lives are more exciting. I have traveled with him and, when possible, our boys go along. We've seen more of the country than most families. I've

seen his profession (selling) grow in stature and his income triple over what we thought possible. The great big difference is that my husband doesn't have to work a 'schedule.' I've found that a salesman who does well sets his own schedule in life; his own income level; and, yes, even decides where and how he wants to live. He's not so restricted by the controls or 'yardsticks' of other professions. I'm glad I married a professional salesman."

Good salesmen enjoy greater security then men in most other professions. When business conditions fall off generally, good managers keep their salesmen because they are the ones who bring in what business might be available under depressed conditions. No company can exist without sales and the salesman is the man who brings in the sales. During the great depression of the 1930's, more salesmen were fully employed 12 months a year than men in any other kind of work.

What does it take to make it big in sales? One maxim, again from *The Salesman—Ambassador of Progress,* accepted by all successful salesmen is: "Selling is the best paid hard work—and the worst paid easy work." Salesmen working on commission are, in effect, in business for themselves. They are paid only when they produce. Even if they draw a small salary or are paid a draw against commissions, they don't last long unless they produce. Few jobs or professions face such a direct challenge—such a direct relationship between income and effort. Hours are seldom fixed and frequently extend beyond eight hours a day. Selling is hard work—definitely not the life for anyone who isn't willing to "put out." The hours and the work pace account for much of the turnover in selling jobs. For example, statistics over more than 30 years indicate that only half of those who start to sell insurance are still selling at the end of one year. After three years, only 20 percent are still at it.

While some salesmen are born—most salesmen, even those with the gift of persuasion, can benefit from objective training.

Selling combines many skills into one profession—psychology, sensitivity to human problems, absorption in human relations, interpersonal communication—plus specific knowledge of the product being sold. Modern, successful selling adopts the by-words—"Selling is serving."

SALES OPPORTUNITIES THAT PAY OFF BIG

Computer hardware

Shemwater-Boldt started as two partners who quit their unimaginative electronic engineering jobs in a big company. The two sensed opportunities for marrying a variety of specialty electronic equipment to the big computers being sold by IBM, Honeywell, and others. Tape-to-card converters, remote input-ting, specialty printers, and character analyzers were just a few pieces of the exotic hardware that were coming off the lines of small, high-technology companies. In the remote Pacific North-west, these companies could sell only by sending one of the of-ficers on occasional trips. There was no service available nearby. So, Dale Shemwater, an electronics engineer, contacted these small, upcoming companies and offered his services as a Techni-cal Sales Representative—more generally known by the title of Manufacturers' Representative. The response was so great, he and Steve Boldt joined forces to form their own sales firm. Now the firm hires four full-time technical salesmen plus two full-time service men and the inevitable office help.

Shemwater-Boldt operates by studying company require-ments and matching these requirements with the machinery they have for sale. They engineer the requirement at times by pointing out to a computing department the savings in time and money possible if they used one or more of their machines. Cost savings provide the opening wedge. Unless one of their machines will cut a company's costs, there's little likelihood of a sale. Shemwater-Boldt acts as a systems analyst. They study a whole system, looking for applications where the equipment they know and understand can increase a company's efficiency. There are no glad-handing, big entertainment bills for buyers, and few really personal relationships. A sale depends on showing a dollars-and-cents improvement in operations, and savings must be dramatic to pay for the investment, usually in only two or three years.

Note the elements that fit together into a successful pattern for Shemwater-Boldt—

High-technology field—Both Dale and Steve graduated in electronics engineering and spent years in design and field service. They understand their own machines—and how they interface with customers' machines. Much of their time is spent working out the bugs that inevitably crop up when their machines are married with a customer's computer. These debugging sessions involve sleeves-rolled-up digging and all-night involvement at times. But, they know their business, their machines, and how to tackle problems.

Stand-alone business—Shemwater-Boldt own their business and contract their sales know-how with specific companies in exchange for an exclusive territory. The companies they represent pay Shemwater-Boldt nothing unless they sell. But, the commission on sales runs as high as 25 percent of the sales price. High—but still less costly for a small company than maintaining its own branch sales office or attempting to sell so far from their home office.

Selling, the key—The partners must sell in both directions. First, they sell their services as technical representatives to producing companies and negotiate contracts fair to both. Second, they sell the products of the companies they represent, often in competition with other representatives selling similar equipment.

Changeable business—Success in selling one company's products may go too far, and Shemwater-Boldt may be dumped by the company. When volume builds to a point, a company may decide to establish its own branch office. With enough volume, branch office expenses may cost less than the commission being paid to Shemwater-Boldt. Or, a company may delete a product from its line—customers for specific units may be limited because of a product's special nature, or a competitor may offer a better product at less money. So, the partners continue to evaluate new products and look into new fields for expansion. Recently, Shemwater-Boldt took on a complete line of specialized numerical-control computers for controlling automated machine tools.

Salesmen look at problems as opportunities, and Shemwater-Boldt continues to expand. The pay is good—Dale Shemwater lives in a waterfront home, moors a huge cabin cruiser at his own dock, and his family drives three cars. Dale's income ranges toward $100,000 annually.

In-house salesmen

Selling pays off inside big companies, too. Not only do sales-oriented executives move up rapidly into executive suites, but they earn high salaries as they advance. When Phil H. took over as sales and service manager for a hydraulic equipment firm, the job involved more service than sales. So, Phil moved into sales for a specialty steel manufacturer. Within one year, by concentrating his efforts strictly on sales, he increased the declining steel division's sales volume by 300 percent. His plans to double sales again within three years project a need for added production capacity. Credit for the increase in sales and profits goes directly to Phil—and he was rewarded with a salary increase that doubled his pay earned as the sales and service manager for the hydraulic firm.

Territory selling

Operating with a sample case and order book, the modern territory salesman closely resembles old-time "drummers" but with a difference—keen competition and sophisticated buyers. Tom F. represents a high quality cutlery manufacturer. Although on the payroll, Tom operates independently and draws commissions only. He pays his own expenses, both for travel and entertainment, and his commission rate allows for such expenses. Such an arrangement forces management decisions on Tom, as he must decide when traveling will pay off and when it won't. Decisions to entertain buyers fall into the same category. Tom operates truly as an independent businessman, making decisions daily on whom to contact for business, how to outfox the competition, the selling approach to each department store buyer, and, of course, how many calls to make and where to concentrate his efforts to meet factory quotas. Many selling opportunities call for similar management decisions.

Tom applies many of the skills he has learned from training sessions and hard-knock experience. Interpersonal communication and an understanding of human nature affect his performance because, as Tom will tell you, "There's very little difference in quality between our knives and our competitions' knives." When product differentiation is slight, personal selling ability, honed to a fine edge by training, really pays off.

PART-TIME SELLING—YOUR KEY TO BIG-TIME MOONLIGHTING PROFITS

Look around—opportunities for you to expand your income through part-time selling exist everywhere.

But, you should be aware of the pitfalls. Part-time selling washes out close to 90 percent of those who start for two main reasons—

Opportunities in part-time selling call for skilled, motivated salesmen.

Goods and services available for part-time selling frequently call for door-to-door selling, one of the most difficult selling environments. Good salesmen with persistence earn fabulous per-hour incomes selling pots and pans or encyclopedias door-to-door. One Business Administration student averaged $17,000 every year for four years while he attended the University.

Despite the inherent problems, the following examples typify the earning capacity of selling part time—

Correspondence Courses—Mail-order schools advertise widely for students for nearly every trade and vocation. Personal follow-ups and sales from inquiries lead to exceptional earnings. There are no "cold calls." A west coast school of drafting, for example, sells a complete, well-designed, and developed course priced at $600. For every course a salesman sells, he earns $85 commission. Selling occurs mainly after dinner because potential students are looking for a way to educate and advance themselves. So, the moonlighting salesman spends two or three hours several nights a week following up on inquiries mailed to him by the home office. Once he signs up a client, the home office handles all training and collections on time-payment plans. All the salesman does is sell the course and he nets an average of $200 each week. Similar opportunities are available for all the large correspondence schools.

Mutual Funds—Salesmen willing to work during the evening hours and on weekends find selling mutual funds part-time profitable and satisfying. First, sales are mainly to professional people and others with cash to invest. Second, calls are follow-ups to inquiries. Third, fund selling usually requires a license and customers respect the salesman as a professional. Commissions are relatively standard at 2 to 4 percent of gross sales which usually run into thousands of dollars.

Real Estate—Weekends and weekday afternoons are key selling times for residential property. So, housewives and moonlighters can sell houses and land while working at their regular jobs. Most states require would-be real estate salesmen to pass an examination to earn a license. Commissions on houses or lots don't happen often, but—wow—when they do, they pay off around 2 percent of the selling price for houses and about 3 percent for lots and land.

Party Plans—Dresses, underclothes, shoes, kitchenware, and household supplies are only a few of the products sold by getting a group together after dinner for a showing. People like parties, and some kitchenware sales plans offer a complete dinner for guests. Party-plan selling is particularly effective with *Tupperware,* an outstanding example. Pathway Products also expanded sales when they switched money-makers, with earnings averaging $10 to $50 per hour of invested time.

SELLING—THE AFTER-50 OPPORTUNITY

Like the merger-displaced executive, men and women over 50 face reduced opportunities. Between the ages of 45 and 50, many men recognize they are not going to make it into the president's chair—time is running out on them. They feel trapped in middle-management or dead-end slots. Yet, many are not ready for retirement just yet. Women may be free from the everyday chores of raising children at close to the same age. Selling offers an "out" for both men and women if they are motivated and willing to work. Maturity and experience become advantages in selling real estate, travel, investments, insurance, technical services, and products—the full line. Resistance to change prevents many unhappy men from going into sales. Yet, there is no future for "obsolete people" trapped in dead-end jobs.

YOUR STEP-BY-STEP GUIDE TO BIG-PROFIT SELLING

Determine first whether your personality can be tuned to selling. You do this through testing. Contact your local state employment service (the address will be in the Yellow Pages of your telephone directory) and ask for counseling assistance. Some people will never make good salesmen. You may find that the counselor can arrange for testing as part of the state services. Or, the counselor will offer you a selection from unbiased testing services for which you will pay. Don't depend on a selling ability test administered by one of the sales training schools. Some of these schools use the test as a device for attracting students and few applicants "fail."

If your test indicates an aptitude and interest in selling, get the best training you can afford *before* tackling your first selling job. You wouldn't attempt to design part of an airplane without engineering training or prescribe medical care without attending medical school. So, don't assume you can sell without training.

Schools offering training in sales, selling methods, practical psychology, and motivation for selling operate principally in two sections: during the day to train industrial and business sales personnel for in-house positions and during evening hours to train ambitious men and women who sense the opportunities and want to get into selling. You'll find a variety of opportunities for sales training in your community. Check these—

Junior college and high school adult education programs offer courses in direct selling, public speaking, psychology of selling, and specialized courses in real estate and investments to help you pass state exams for a sales license. If you live near a major college, investigate its day and evening class schedules for courses related to sales training.

Join one of the Toastmaster clubs to gain experience in speaking and confidence in expressing yourself.

Investigate one of the privately operated schools specializing in training for sales. One major school is *Sales Training, Inc.* (STI) with head offices in Seattle, Washington. STI began teaching salesmanship only 13 years ago. Now it operates 17 branches in the United States and Canada. Nationally, STI graduates 2,000 trained salesmen from their "Whole-Man Program" every year. The school addresses much of its course work to positive attitude and confidence building, motivational training, and mental conditioning. Role playing in simulated selling situations affords experience, and these sessions are taped for playback on TV so that students can see their own mistakes and correct them.

Success Motivation Institute operates nationally through franchises. SMI's approach is aimed at building confidence and motivation to carry through in sales and other activities.

Dale Carnegie Schools offer sales training as one of their options in addition to executive training.

Look for these and other schools in the Yellow Pages. Your local state employment counselor may suggest another avenue for special training rather than a full program.

Read from the hundreds of books published on just about every element of selling. Check your local library. Behavioral research and applications have laid new foundations for understanding and teaching salesmanship.

Select your selling opportunity only after carefully analyzing several from leads in your newspaper classified section, state employment service, private employment agency, or individual referral. Check into these aspects and evaluate them carefully—

Will you be given additional on-the-job training? Insurance companies, mutual-fund houses, and part-time sales organizations often provide specialized training and aids for selling their own product or service.

Will you be comfortable selling the product or service? Can you tell your friends about your selling activities with pride? If you can't, you should look for a different opportunity.

Will you be required to buy inventory or pay a franchise fee? Any opportunity that requires a substantial cash investment should be checked with the Better Business Bureau, your banker, and operators in other areas—references furnished by the franchiser.

What are the earning possibilities? Check these just as carefully as you would your own business opportunity. Develop high and low projections, then check your answers with actual earnings from salesmen in the same line of selling.

Preparation through training, selection from opportunities through detailed evaluation, and sticking to your plan will improve the odds of your success in selling a thousandfold.

9

How to Build a Lifetime Treasury that Delivers Automatic Dividends, Year After Year

Do you have a built-in key to personal and financial success?

Can nearly anyone, regardless of his monetary worth or station in life, achieve the kind of success that brings him money, influence, and happiness?

Is there a magic system you can set up that will point the way to wealth-building opportunities for you automatically, year after year?

Research indicates "Yes" is the answer to all three questions.

"Success is a state of mind," William Lawson, Chief of Public Information of the California State Department of Hu-

From Hal D. Steward, *Money Making Secrets of the Millionaires* (West Nyack, N.Y., Parker Publishing Company, Inc., 1972)

man Resources Development once said, "and once the state is acquired a man's achievements can be limitless."

Bill Lawson should know. He emigrated to the United States from Borneo in 1959 with a small amount of savings in the bank. Within 10 years after his arrival in the U.S., he'd established a successful public relations and advertising firm and had achieved a high position in California's State Government.

Bill Lawson knew what he wanted. He established his goals, he had an overpowering desire to achieve them, and he set about reaching them without regard to luck—he made his own luck.

"Shallow men believe in luck," said Ralph Waldo Emerson. There isn't any luck, as Bill Lawson knows, along the path a man follows to personal and financial success. What is along that path to success are hours of study, well-conceived and executed plans, specific goals, and lots of hard work.

Why do we all want to achieve success?

Let's admit it—we all crave attention. We want to be important, immortal. We want to do things that will make people exclaim, "Isn't he wonderful?"

The best and most constructive way for you to gain attention, to acquire your piece of immortality, is to achieve success.

Let's take, for instance, the circumstances of James Joseph Ling, once one of America's richest men. But in early 1946 he was just out of the U.S. Navy, had no occupational skill, and little money.

Ling decided the way he'd begin his climb to success would be to become a licensed electrical engineer. So he read and memorized two books: *The Electrical Engineer's Handbook* and *The National Electrical Code.* On his second try he passed the city of Dallas electrical engineering examination. He was 22 at the time.

But Jim Ling didn't want to be an electrical engineer working for someone else—he wanted to be an electrical contractor running his own business.

So, with $3,000 that he'd saved from his Navy pay in

World War II, Ling opened his own contracting business. That was his beginning; within 20 years he'd become a multi-millionaire.

What, then, were the elements of Ling's success?

First, it was, as he admits, the desire to succeed, and succeed rapidly.

Second, his staying power, "It's the staying power that makes the difference between winners and losers," he said.

The point is that nothing can stymie a man with the desire, the determination, to succeed.

But, at this point, you're saying to yourself, "How can I relate my circumstances to these wealthy men and women I've read about in this book? Here I am a guy with practically nothing in the bank and I owe money on my house and car."

Well, those were the circumstances of the men and women in this book when they began their climb to success. That's why their stories were selected to tell in making points, and laying out a blueprint that you too can use for your own financial advancement. What they have done, you can do.

Ken Riley, for instance, said there were four major elements that enabled him to become a millionaire. They are, he said:

1. A burning desire and driving ambition to be wealthy.

2. A tolerant and understanding wife, Melinda, without whom I couldn't have succeeded so rapidly.

3. A book, *Law of Success* by Napoleon Hill.

4. An inspirational record, "Strangest Secret" by Earl Nightingale, distributed by Success Motivation Institute, Inc., Waco, Texas.

But where you ask, did Ken Riley get the money to start his climb to financial success?

Simply put, he earned it and saved it until he had enough to make a down payment on his first piece of real estate property. Riley worked in the stock room of a retail store, he worked on construction projects, and he took jobs wherever he could find them to earn extra money.

Then, when he'd saved enough, he used his savings for the down payment on the first house he constructed. When it was finished he sold it at a profit. He used the profit from that sale to make the down payment on a larger property. This was the way he entered the general contracting business—he kept pyramiding his investments.

Ken Riley's fortune formula worked for him—he insists it'll work for anyone who'll adopt it.

Honolulu's William Koon Kee Mau followed a path similar to Riley's in his rise to great wealth.

Bill Mau started his career as an elevator operator, then he worked in an advertising agency, and finally obtained a U.S. Civil Service job. But these were only progressive steps in his climb to wealth. All the while he worked at these jobs he saved as much of his salary as he could, and he was always on the lookout for opportunities. His first independent investment was a hamburger stand that he started with money he'd saved plus money he was able to borrow from friends. At first he kept his civil service job and worked at it by day while he manned his hamburger stand at night.

But the essential point about Bill Mau's career is that he always knew what he wanted and he refused to permit anything to interfere with the achievement of his objectives.

And neither Bill Mau nor any of the other men and women whose success stories have been told in this book ever permitted themselves to entertain the possibility of failure.

Let's, as an example, look at the career of Patrick Henry, American patriot, who failed repeatedly, but never accepted failure. There is a difference between failing at something you attempt and being a failure. The difference is that the failure, once he's failed, never again attempts to succeed. This wasn't Patrick Henry's way.

By the time he was 23, Patrick Henry had failed twice as a storekeeper and once as a farmer. But he refused to quit.

"What can I do to make myself a success?" he asked. The answer: become a lawyer; but how, without time or money, could he study law? He had a wife, four children, and burdensome debts.

Nevertheless, Patrick Henry borrowed a set of law books and studied them relentlessly. Then he traveled to Williamsburg, the colonial capital of Virginia, and presented himself for examination. He passed and was admitted to the Virginia Bar.

The remainder of Patrick Henry's career is history—he went from success to greater success the rest of his life. And what success he achieved; the man who refused to accept failure.

So, the important question for you, as one who wants to make a success of himself, is whether you really want to succeed. If your answer is "Yes," then you also need to answer these questions with honesty:

How strong is my desire to succeed?

Do I have enough personal drive to succeed?

Can I discipline myself constantly to assure myself that I'm doing everything that I must do to achieve my goal?

Will I do what's necessary—in time, study, working—to achieve my goal?

If you can answer "Yes" to these, and you mean it, then you have the ingredients of a successful man or woman. But there is an additional ingredient that you must have to succeed—staying power. You must be able to accept setbacks without giving up; you mustn't let temporary failures force you to give up; and, no matter what, you must keep your eye on and direct all your efforts toward the goal you've set for yourself.

These are the qualities that separate the successful man and woman from the failures. You must either have them or develop them.

Ed Robinson, of Oceanside, California, developed these qualities quickly and used them to amass wealth for himself in a rather small city.

When Ed Robinson began his climb to success he was in his

mid-40's, he had a mortgaged home, an automobile he was making monthly payments on, and two children he was helping put through college.

On top of these drawbacks, Ed Robinson reacted counter to the millions of men and women who each year leave small cities for metropolitan ones because they believe their hometowns offer them scant opportunity.

Nevertheless, Robinson's success story proves, at least in his instance, that they could have found success at home if they had had the desire, ambition, and personal drive to go after it.

How did Ed Robinson achieve his success? How did he set up the magic system to find the wealth-building opportunities he needed?

He simply applied for a job as an insurance salesman, got it, and set about becoming the most successful insurance man in his city. And he did this by establishing goals for himself and then setting out, regardless of obstacles, to achieve them.

The method used by Robinson didn't require money to get him started on his success ladder. He succeeded by becoming aware of the wealth-building opportunities around him.

You must be alert for wealth opportunities around you or that come your way.

How, you ask, do I find wealth-building opportunities? These are some of the ways:

1. Look for possibilities in the Business Opportunities columns in the classified ad section of your daily newspapers. And don't overlook your regional and neighborhood weekly newspapers. They, too, often contain opportunities that may appeal to you.

2. Talk to businessmen. Ask their advice. Ask them to suggest opportunities they may know of but can't take advantage of themselves.

3. Read widely. Become a regular patron of your public library. Get to know the librarian and ask her to keep an eye out for the new books on business and finance that may interest you.

4. Read business publications. *The Wall Street Journal, Business Week, Nation's Business, Barron's, Fortune, Success Unlimited,* and so on. If you can't afford to subscribe to them, go to your library regularly and read them. You'll find in them an endless number of wealth-building opportunities.

And above all, make use of your friends—particularly those in business who understand financing, business management, and how to locate and develop wealth-building opportunities.

If you believe you need to increase your knowledge of business and finance, enroll in college and university night courses in your area. Take courses in business administration, accounting, marketing, salesmanship, real estate, banking, investments and so on.

On the other hand, if you can't attend resident courses on a regular basis, enroll in correspondence courses such as those offered by these schools:

LaSalle Extension University, 417 South Dearborn Street, Chicago, Illinois 60605

International Correspondence Schools, Scranton, Pennsylvania 18515

Both of these schools will permit you to pay for your courses on the monthly installment plan. Write them a letter, tell them what your goal is, and they'll provide you with information on what courses you should take in your efforts to achieve it.

If you've read this far, you know every successful person mentioned in this book did two essential things to achieve wealth:

1. They made up their minds, and developed an overwhelming desire to achieve wealth because they knew the comfortable, satisfying status of wealth was precisely what they wanted.

2. They wanted wealth so earnestly that they were willing to do something everyday of their lives to help achieve success.

These essentials apply equally to women.

Linda Sinay operates her own advertising agency in Los Angeles. In five years, she developed her agency from an at-home operation with no capital to a current annual billing of more than $1 million a year.

What is Linda Sinay's success formula? In her own words, it's this:

> I learned early I couldn't work for anybody. I had to do it myself. I still do. And I try to hire people just like that. There's no mystique. I'm not a witch. But I know if you have confidence, know who you are and work hard, you can make it. It's there to be had.

It's there for you, too.

Laurie Hancock also knew it was there, and she began to reach for it as a high school student in Thief River Falls, Minnesota.

If there was one day in her life that can be pinpointed as the precise day Laurie Hancock began her climb to wealth, it was the day she was selected the outstanding business student in her high school and appointed after-school secretary to her principal.

Mrs. Hancock couldn't afford to go to college, but she had a natural aptitude for business and an unrelenting desire to achieve success.

Upon graduation from high school, she applied to the president of the Union State Bank in Thief River Falls for the job as the bank president's secretary. Her high school principal, for whom she'd been a part-time secretary, gave her high recommendations for the job. She got it.

In her job with the bank, Laurie Hancock quickly learned

about banking, how businesses were financed, what business-men needed to do to obtain loans for the expansion of the businesses or to start new ones.

"I learned a great deal from my boss because I saw problems and situations through his eyes and the psychology with which he dealt with them," she said. "I learned so much, in fact, it was an 'on-the-job' college education."

But being a secretary was only a beginning for Laurie Hancock.

Later when she became involved in business on her own, she applied the age-old principle "to be a success, discover a need and fill it."

Laurie Hancock understood this to mean, as have other successful men and women, that if you find people want something they don't have, then you can become rich by providing them with it. Men and women have made themselves multimillionaires following this principle—frozen foods, canned baby food, wash-and-wear clothing—the list is endless.

In Laurie Hancock's case it was manufacturing better and more attractive outdoor redwood furniture.

She challenged her mind with these two questions as she designed and manufactured better furniture: "Is what I have in mind better, stronger, lovelier, more practical and useful? Does it provide a chance for greater returns, or insure an easier way of life?"

When she got the answer "Yes" to both questions, then she knew she was on the right path.

Laurie Hancock had an all-powerful desire to achieve a specific goal. She achieved it and today enjoys the comforts that wealth can bring.

Still another person who had that all-power desire to achieve a specific goal is G. Ralph Bartolme. In his advice to those who want to duplicate his success he said, "You must carry through no matter what temptations might be presented to deter you."

Bartolme began his climb to success by getting a job with

the U.S. Internal Revenue Service. On that job he learned that one method that could be used to achieve great personal wealth, despite the U.S. tax structure, was for a person to go into business for himself where capital gains are possible or work for a company and share in its prosperity through stock options.

"After a year-and-a-half with the Internal Revenue Service I felt I'd learned all I could from it," Bartolme said. "It became obvious that the Government can give you experience and security, but no wealth."

Bartolme, like Laurie Hancock, had obtained a salaried job that would give him the experience and teach him the techniques he'd need later to succeed in his own business. It's an effective technique and one that you, the reader, should consider in your own plans.

In looking for such a job to start your career that will lead to wealth, Bartolme believes you must do three things:

1. Become a part of a growth industry; that is, connect with a firm that is forging ahead in such fields as pollution and environmental control, electronics, chemicals, plastics, nuclear energy, and the like.

2. Seek out an expanding company, one that is known as a pace-setter in its field.

3. Check for progressive management; make certain the company you join has a management team known for its enlightened leadership, modern-thinking, and development of executive talent.

Once you've joined an expanding company in a growth industry, Bartolme advises, you should work by the job, not by the clock; ask intelligent questions of those above you so that you can learn as much as you can quickly about the business; and volunteer whenever possible for the odd assignment—particularly the one your associates shun.

These are the techniques that have worked for Ralph Bartolme; they'll also work for you. Try them.

But, you must guard against defeatism.

You've heard many people say: "It just isn't possible to make a fortune anymore with high taxes, inflation, government controls, and, furthermore, there aren't the opportunities there used to be."

Hogwash!

There are more opportunities today for the ambitious men and women than there have ever been in the history of the United States. People have more money to spend, they have more time in which to enjoy themselves, and they want new and innovative products, recreational facilities, and whatever else money will buy to make their lives more enjoyable.

There is still another way to make your capital grow—invest it in stocks. I'm not recommending that you put all your money in stocks, only that you consider them as an investment for part of your wealth-building activity.

Finally, these are the five steps you must take to start yourself on your path to riches:

1. Begin this very moment, right now, to think of yourself as a success. Don't daydream that you're a success, but think of yourself as one in a practical sense. If you think of yourself as a success, you'll do and act as a successful man or woman—this will start your program of growth to riches.

2. Get a sheet of paper and list all the pluses and minuses—the positives and negatives—that can affect your pathway to riches. These items should include your education, your special knowledge, your experience, your finances, and every practical move that could be made either for or against your plan.

3. Now arrange the material you've collected into a sequence of progress. This means that what you have in mind—your goal—will have to follow from a logical sequence. So, list the steps you'll have to take to reach your goal.

4. Fix on your goal. Concentrate your interest on precisely what you want to accomplish. Do you strive for a better job, do you want to start a business of your own? Decide what your objective is and stick to it.

5. Now take two sheets of paper. Put a heading at the top of one, "Points that Favor the Achievement of My Goal." And on the other put "Points Against the Achievement of My Goal." This will enable you to decide what obstacles you must overcome on your path to wealth as well as tell you what your attributes are that will help you achieve it. Be honest in making these lists. Then keep them for constant reference. From time to time as you develop and move forward toward your goal, you'll want to switch the items from one page to another. For instance, if one of the points against the achievement of your goal is lack of experience, you'll switch that later to a favorable point when you've gained the needed experience.

In the years that it took to gather the material for this book, the Wealth-Building Secrets of the millionaires have come under close scrutiny. All of their ideas, plans, decisions and devices have been examined and are now available for you to use. The choice is yours.

Never doubt that your dreams are within your reach. Our fast-paced world cries out for new ideas, and the men and women who work to transform ideas into reality are handsomely rewarded. You have it within your power to be one of these men or women.

But first you must believe it. You must grasp your destiny and never let it go. If you do, you too will join the ranks of the winners—the place where you belong.

Good Luck.

10

How to Turn Your Second Income Venture into a Lifetime Fortune

As you develop your second income bonanza, you should know how to do four important things that will guarantee increased profits and greater enjoyment. They are:

1. Pay less taxes.
2. Profit from profits.
3. Put fun into your money-making.
4. Steadily increase your income.

Knowing how to do these things will help you venture into a lifetime fortune, as the chapter title implies.

First, though, a piece of advice: Make this book your constant companion in all the stages of the development and growth of your enterprise. One reading can steer you to the right endeavor and get you started, but the second and third readings—

From Scott Witt, *Second Income Money Makers* (West Nyack, N.Y., Parker Publishing Company, Inc., 1975) and spot checks on particular subjects—can bring out vital business-building information you did not detect the first time around.

And don't limit your re-reading to the chapter or chapters that deal with the specific enterprise you've chosen. Advice and tips concerning one business can frequently be applied to many other types of business, so that by becoming thoroughly familiar with the entire book you will be well-versed in the field of building personal wealth with a second income project.

UTILIZE TAX ADVANTAGES

If you've been on a salary all your life and have had your income tax withheld from your weekly paychecks, you may have a mighty pleasant surprise coming once you enter your own business. That surprise is in the form of new deductions that will allow you to keep a larger share of your income.

Perhaps, like Francine P., who operates a real estate brokerage, you will be operating your business from home. Francine uses the former den as her office. It costs her no more to operate her home than before she started the business, but she nevertheless is allowed to deduct part of her home-operating costs as legitimate business expenses.

It's important to remember this fact:

Every deduction means tax-free income.

By operating her business from home, Francine is able to include a $729.17 deduction on her income tax return. It's the same as putting $729.17 in her pocket without having to pay taxes on it. That's why all business people look for all of the legitimate deductions they can possibly take.

Consider these deductions

No matter where your business is located—at home or in outside quarters—there are typical deductions you will probably be able to take. These include most expenses that are incurred for the operation of your enterprise.

Examine each of the items in the following list for possible deductions on your own return. Don't fall into the trap that has caused many businessmen not to take full advantage of the deduction and depreciation items available to them. The government says overpayment of taxes (not taking enough deductions) is one of the major causes of business failure.

Here's the list:

Salaries and wages (but not your own)

Advertising

Depreciation of property and equipment

Licenses and regulatory fees

Incidental supplies and materials

Dues to business associations

Training

Business taxes

Local transportation

Overnight travel

Entertainment

Rent

Heat, light, and power

Bad debts

Insurance premiums

Interest on indebtedness

PUT YOUR SURPLUS CASH TO WORK

Not long after your second income enterprise is launched, you may find yourself with considerably more money than you need. What will you do with it?

"No problem!" says the average person. "I can think of a million ways to spend it."

Sure you can, but you'll have to agree that using the money to make *more* money is a better idea. Certainly, as the extra income starts to roll in, enjoy some of the luxuries you've never been able to partake of before. Take a cruise, buy a boat, give your wife a new wardrobe, latch on to a summer cottage.

But if you've followed the instructions in this book, and your endeavor is a continuous money-maker, the cash will keep on rolling in . . . and what do you do with it then?

You start building a fortune.

You do it by investing your surplus cash. You put your

money into investments that will either (a) earn interest or (b) achieve growth in value.

Here's how eight persons are investing *their* surplus cash:

Long-term bank certificates. Irving K. likes long-term bank certificates because he can sock his money away with absolutely no worry about its safety and earn the highest legal rate of interest.

Mutual funds. Allen H. puts his surplus cash into no-load mutual funds—the kind which have no sales or redemption charges. "I know that in the long run the stock market is headed up, and I decided to have experts choose my stocks for me," Allen explains. "And that's what a mutual fund does—provide you with part ownership of a portfolio of carefully-selected securities."

Rental real estate. Anna M. uses the profits from her in-home beauty shop to put down payments on small apartment houses. "Once I make the down payment," Anna says, "the buildings pay for themselves out of the rent roll. While they are being paid off, their value grows because of constantly rising real estate prices—so my fortune climbs two ways!"

Second mortgages. Henry R. puts his money into second mortgages. He's following the advice contained in *Mortgage Your Way to Wealth: The Principle of Supplemental Real Estate Financing* by Joseph L. Steinberg, published by Parker Publishing Company, Inc. Henry was attracted to Mr. Steinberg's instructions on how to start with as little as $1,500 and earn an accumulated return of more than 56 percent.

Art. Jean S. believes in art as an investment, and that's where her surplus cash goes. After taking several art courses, she began buying the works of lesser-known artists, but works that she was convinced would grow in value. Most of them have. "I've invested a total of $62,000 over the past five years," Jean reports, "and my holdings were recently appraised at $118,000." That's a 90 percent growth factor for the five-year period.

Land. Ed H.'s surplus cash from his sandwich shop goes into vacation land. Not for *his* vacations, mind you; this land will be bought in the future by others as sites for their vacation homes. Ed lives in Vermont and has seen land values skyrocket over the years because of people from other states who want to build second homes there. Ed buys up large parcels as they become available and holds them for appreciation in value. He plans to divide them into lots and sell the lots individually some time in the future.

Municipal bonds. John E. doesn't need more cash. "No way," he states. "More income just means putting me in a higher tax bracket—and I'm already in a 60 percent bracket." So John does what many others in his circumstances do. He invests in municipal bonds. They pay lower interest than many other investments, but the return is tax-free. "And then I use that interest to buy *more* municipal bonds!" John adds.

Antiques. Lucy J. has always loved antiques, and when her interior decorating business started to provide her with surplus cash, she began to furnish her own home with early American items and some foreign antiques. "Other people buy new furniture that drops drastically in value the minute it comes out of the store," Lucy states. "But my furniture increases in value by 10 percent–25 percent per year."

COMBINE PLEASURE WITH BUSINESS

Two of the people in these examples are profiting from their investments in a twofold way. The first, naturally, is in the form of cash. But Jean S. and Lucy J. are also pursuing personal interests with their investments—Jean with art and Lucy with antiques. You, too, can combine pleasure with your second income activities. In other words, why not choose an enterprise that allows you to pursue your hobby or pastime?

You can choose a hobby-related job or business because

your knowledge in the field makes you more qualified for prompt earnings than if you were starting from scratch. But there's an added benefit, and that, of course, is the fact that you'll get more *enjoyment* out of what you're doing.

There are hundreds of examples of people who have capitalized on their hobbies to build sizable fortunes, but one should suffice.

Gene B. has always been a motorcycle enthusiast. As a teenager, he used to race them, and then after he was married, he and his wife took some cross-country motorcycle tours. As the popularity of motorcycling grew, Gene became convinced of the need in his community for a motorcycle sales and repair shop. With borrowed cash, he obtained the franchise for a well-known brand, stocked a vacant store, and operated it with the assistance of hired help while he was at his regular job. His profit the first year was $11,000—and now he owns three outlets and is drawing more than $60,000 annually from them.

Review your pastimes for profit opportunities

Webster defines *pastime* as something that makes time pass agreeably. We all have one or more pastimes, and there's no reason in the world why you shouldn't look to one of yours first in considering a second income.

If, for example, your interest is reading books, you might like to do any of the following:

- Run a bookshop.
- Serve as a part-time librarian.
- Deal in rare books.
- Review books for the local newspaper.
- Type manuscripts for authors.
- Proofread for publishers.
- Compile indexes for publishers and authors.
- Write books.

- Be a substitute literature teacher.
- Become a part-time publisher.

Many people have done these things. Sometimes the profit has been greater than the pleasure, and sometimes it's been the other way around—but in all cases, there has been a goodly measure of both. So examine *your* favorite pastime and consider the many opportunities it offers!

CONSTANTLY SEEK TO UPGRADE YOUR SECOND JOB

When you land a well-paying part-time position are you then satisfied? Not for long, if you're the second income expert you should have become. You'll be constantly seeking to upgrade that job. It's the person who is never satisfied who moves ahead most rapidly. There are several ways you can give yourself a big boost.

Increase your value to your employer

If you can show your employer how to make more money— or if you, yourself, are able to make more money *for* him—you have become a more valuable employee, and this should be reflected in your pay.

Andy Q. moonlighted as an early morning newspaper deliveryman, driving a route that took him through several communities. He could see two possible ways to increase the pay on that job. One was to extend his route, but that would take more time and would, in fact, cut into his regular workday.

The second alternative was to sell more newspapers to his regular customers. Andy conferred with his boss and offered to call on each of his customers during his off-hours and suggest they order a metropolitan newspaper to go along with the suburban paper they were already receiving.

Andy's boss agreed to pay Andy a continuing commission

for each sale he made. Andy was able to sign up half of the customers on his regular route—and now, with very little extra work, he is earning 25 percent more.

Move to a larger company

There are times when you'll find you've reached the top of the rung in the company where you are working. (This happens with second jobs just as in full-time employment.) There's nowhere to go, it seems, and the only raises you can expect are those that result from cost-of-living adjustments.

The only course of action in such a case is to seek similar employment with a firm better able to meet the type of salary you seek.

That, in fact, is what Alicia N. did. Alicia was well paid as an advertising writer for a department store in her town, working several hours each day. Well paid, but still not what she knew her talents were worth. The store, however, was unable to give her any more merit increases.

"The manager told me he had already overextended his advertising budget, so he was going to have to cut down, not increase, his expenses. I could see no future there, so . . . "

Alicia started looking. She lived in a small city, and there were not very many companies that were large enough to afford advertising personnel. But Alicia knew that several could very much stand an improvement in the quality of their ads—even if it didn't take a person working 20 hours per week to do it.

So, she contacted several retail outlets and offered to work as an advertising consultant on a continuing fee basis. She now devotes only a few hours per week to each of the assignments—but is totaling more than double what she used to earn from the department store.

"And the really surprising part of it all," she reports, "is that the department store manager saw what I've been doing and *he* has hired me as a consultant—at my standard fee, which is considerably more, per hour spent, than what he'd been paying me when I worked there before!"

You can make a similar move

Alicia's story demonstrates that there is more than one way of moving up. In your case, you may choose a much simpler route; if there is a better job open with another company, your best move may be to accept it.

Or, as in Alicia's case, when no obvious openings exist—you can wedge an opening or two where none existed before. Show a company how you can help it make more money and it will eagerly accept your offer.

Train for a better position '

People have been doing this for years in their regular jobs, why not in second-income positions as well? It may very well be that in your line of spare-time work there is room for advancement provided you receive some additional training.

Louis C. worked as a night-time engineer for a local radio station. His job was to repair tape recorders and amplifiers, and keep an eye on the transmitter. If the transmitter broke down, he would call the chief engineer in to make the necessary adjustments or repairs.

Lou had a third-class radiotelephone operator's license. This allowed him to take readings from the dials on the transmitter, but not to make major adjustments or alterations.

One day, dissatisfied with his rate of pay, he sent away for literature on a correspondence course that guaranteed students would pass the test for a first-class license upon completion. Lou took the course (it cost $375) and had his license within six months. Now he is able to do most transmitter repairs by himself, saving his employer money. And because he has become more valuable to the radio station, he is being paid more. The additional $30 per week had his course paid off in 13 weeks and now, as Lou says, "It's pure gravy; same hours, but more pay."

GUIDE THE EXPANSION OF YOUR BUSINESS

If you're like most people who start a spare-time business, you have, in the back of your mind, a private goal: You would like eventually to be able to quit your job and delve into your business full time. And why not? After your business becomes successful, you might be actually *losing* money by holding on to your job. In such a case, your time would be more valuable devoted to the business—and every dollar you earn on the job might mean two dollars less earned in the business.

There are, in fact, a number of advantages to switching your business from a part-time to a full-time basis. Here are some of them:

- Greater earnings potential.
- You're available to make emergency decisions.
- You have greater control over the day-to-day operations.
- More of your income is subject to income tax deductions.
- You can set your own working schedule.
- You are not limited to established vacation periods.
- Your business can grow faster.
- You can establish a self-employment retirement program.

These are advantages worth thinking about, particularly since most of the businesses you learn about in this book can be operated either part-time or full-time.

Know when to make the change

"But how can I tell," you inquire, "when it's safe to give up my job and leap into the business as a sole source of income?" An understandable question, because many people are rightfully concerned about giving up seeming security in their jobs for what might appear to be the more risky world of business.

Studies of personal business across the country have shown how and when people have made that all-important transition. From the most successful changeovers, here are some guidelines that you can follow in making your own decision.

It is time to give serious consideration to going full-time when:

- Your business is putting more money in your pocket than your job is.
- The company has shown steady growth, month by month, for more than two years.
- All signs point to continued growth and greater demand for your products or services.
- Your own enthusiasm for the business is greater than your interest in your job.
- You know you are losing business or profits by devoting only part time to your enterprise.
- You have the support of your closest family members in making the change.

All of these factors should be present before you seriously think about dropping the job for the business. If one or more are absent, problems could lie ahead, so wait until you have all six factors in your favor.

Move ahead with gusto

By following these guidelines, you can make the transition with confidence or even, as was the case with Jim T., with *gusto*.

Jim had developed a thriving mail order business in which he sold do-it-yourself parts for customizing cars . . . items car-owners couldn't usually find in nearby auto stores.

He had run small ads in a number of special interest and

general interest magazines, had developed a series of mailing pieces and mini-catalogs, and had built up quite a good customer list.

It was when he filed an income tax return showing a clear profit of $17,000 that Jim first thought of devoting full-time to it. That was $2,000 more than he was earning as an office manager with an insurance firm.

"Of course, my main consideration was that I'd be actually cutting my pay in half by giving up the job . . . at least at first. Between job and business, I earned $32,000 that year, and if my business showed no growth, all I'd be earning the next year would be $17,000."

That's why the other factors in the guideline are so important. In Jim's case, the mail order business was not only paying more than his job, but it also was showing steady growth. He had the figures to prove it, and these provided a good indication that the growth would continue. So Jim did not have to be concerned that his income would be limited to the $17,000 he earned as a part-timer. He already knew that his enthusiasm for the business was greater than his interest in the office job, for he generally couldn't wait for five o'clock to roll around so he could get home and open the day's orders, send out the packages, and make his nightly bank deposit.

He realized that with more time, he could place more advertising and be able to handle more orders, something the hours spent on the job had prevented.

Convincing his wife, Martha, that giving up the job was the right move did not pose a major obstacle. The profits from the business had already financed the down payment on a new home for them and provided several luxurious vacations . . . and she was convinced that even better things lay ahead.

Thus Jim met all the important criteria. He *did* go full-time, and the very next year he exceeded the income he had earned previously from *both* job and business.

"It's a decision I've never regretted making," he said.

ENJOY THE FRUITS OF YOUR LABOR

You have some pleasant surprises ahead. Your second income bonanza is going to do a lot more for you than you expect. Many other people have been happily surprised at new lives and lifestyles made possible by the additional dollars flowing into their pockets.

This expanded income has enabled them to do things they had never even considered in the past. Even though your goal may be to build a nest egg for your children's education, or to obtain the money for a new home—the continuing success of your second income activity will bring many other rewards into your life.

Here are some of the things second income entrepreneurs have been doing with their new-found surplus cash—money-uses that are *over and above* their original goals:

- Extended foreign travel
- Purchase of a sailing yacht
- Ownership of private airplane
- Sizable donations to charity
- Condominium at a ski resort
- Summer home abroad
- Rearing of foster children
- Extensive art and book collections
- _____
- _____
- _____

Why the blank spaces? So that you can list some items of pure luxury that you would like to accomplish after your main money-making goals are met. Fine. Send the kids to college, but as the money continues to come in, *reward yourself,* too! Splurge. Give yourself some luxuries. With the success of your second income enterprise, you will deserve them. And perhaps help others with your wealth, too.

LEARN TO APPORTION YOUR NEW-FOUND WEALTH

Chris and Sue W. started their second income enterprise—a home-based antique and curio shop—with the goal of paying off a major indebtedness they had incurred due to the serious illness of a family member. $7,500 was owed. Within the first year, it was fully paid off.

"We were enjoying the business so much, though, that we naturally kept on with it—and the profits not only continued to pour in, they increased as our reputation grew," Sue relates. "So now we were faced with a surplus flow of cash far beyond our needs."

Chris carries the story from there. "We sat down one day and decided we'd better figure out how to make sensible use of all that money. We set up sort of a budget—the kind the government prepares each year—with percentage figures on what portion of our extra money should go where."

Here's what their "budget" looked like:

Investments	50%
Donations	20%
Personal luxuries	10%
Vacation fund	20%

Thus, with $17,500 in net profit after taxes, $8,750 went into various investments, $3,500 was given to selected charitable and religious organizations, $1,750 was spent on personal luxuries such as shop equipment for Chris and furs for Sue, and $3,500 was used for a South American tour.

Your own budget will, of course, be somewhat different—

depending on your personal interests and aims. But do prepare one, because it will assure the sensible use of your funds and will also give you added motivation.

THIS IS YOUR KIT OF WEALTH-BUILDING SECRETS

Kits are "in" these days. Hobbyists by the thousands are building TV's and stereo tuners with electronics kits, or tables and bookcases with furniture kits, or even boats and airplanes with nautical and aeronautical kits. Think of this book as your Wealth-Building kit. It enables you, with the raw materials you already have at hand, to build your own personal fortune.

But as with any kit, the final result is up to *you*. The instructions are here and the "parts" (the items used in your business) are readily available, but it is up to you to put them together.

As you proceed, continue to use these pages as your assembly manual. They will help you win the same kind of success achieved by the people in the many examples that have been included for your guidance.

Yes, the entire kit is ready and waiting for you. Start using it . . . *right now*.

11

How to Use Your Lifetime Treasury of Wealth-Building Secrets Every Day of the Year

Up to this point you've read about making big money through part-time enterprises. Now it's time to find ways to take some of the profits made in your part-time business and make them work even harder. You can do this by investing. These investments can be conventional ones like real estate, stocks, bonds, mutual funds and others, or unconventional ones that you can get into easily with little money, yet still return a good profit.

This chapter will look into some of the ins and outs of investing to show you how to make investments that will propel you to even greater riches.

From Duane G. Newcomb, *Spare-Time Fortune Guide* (West Nyack, N.Y., Parker Publishing Company, Inc., 1973)

HOW TO LOOK FOR THE RIGHT KIND OF INVESTMENTS

Not all investment opportunities will be right for you. Some will require more money than you want to invest, others will take too much time to manage, still others will be too risky. Here are some factors to consider:

1. A good investment will be one that allows you to start with what you have available. This includes the amount of money you have to invest, the time you want to spend, the knowledge you have, the equipment you need and all else.

2. A good investment will operate, at least part of the time, under its own momentum automatically. That is, you will not have to work at it as you do an ordinary business, putting in regular hours and specified periods of time.

3. A good investment will contain a limited amount of risk. All investments contain some risk—some, however, are reasonable, while others are wild gambles.

George and Eric Templeton of Houston, Texas, are good examples of both of these. George and Eric were brothers with two thousand dollars each to invest. George weighed the risk of each investment, then put $1000 in mutual funds and $1000 in tube testers leased to retail stores.

Eric, on the other hand, backed two brothers who believed they could strike it rich mining gold in Idaho. The rest he invested in a 1000 mph rapid transit system advanced as the lifetime dream of a local engineer.

George's mutual fund returned almost 7 percent a year, the tube tester investment 22 percent. Eric, however, never heard from the gold mining brothers again, and had to sue the engineer to get part of his money back.

4. A good investment also feels right to you. This is hard to define, but after looking over all the available material and considering the possibilities, it simply seems to be the right course. In your investing career you will find some investments that fit the other three criteria listed here, but simply feel wrong for you. While this may be unscientific, you'll be wise to avoid those investments and consider only those you can actually get excited about.

WHERE TO FIND SMALL CASH INVESTMENTS

As soon as your part-time business starts producing extra, uncommitted cash, you should immediately start an investment program to get that money working again. The big problem for most small investors is where to find $50, $100, $200 and even $500 investments that produce good returns. Actually, they are all around you. There are several areas in this section that will help you get started. Here are some to consider:

Recreation or spare-time rentals

What a wide open field this is—recreational rental investments include bicycles, snowmobiles, motorcycles, trailers, campers, canoes, ATV's and similar items. A recreational rental investment, however, is quite distinct from a recreational rental business. You simply buy the rental units, then place them in various locations for others to rent.

Douglas Toms, a Seattle, Washington businessman who quit his $7000 a year warehouse job and parlayed a borrowed $75 into an extremely lucrative $80,000 a year making Indian Tepees on special order, was looking for a safe way to pyramid his fortune without risk. One day Douglas happened to be reading a magazine article about the growing bicycle craze when he suddenly realized that there was extra money to be made from this sport. The next day he lined up a number of filling station operators who would let him place tandem bicycles on their lots for rent. The operator was to provide the lot, take care of the bicycles, keep records and rent them out. For this he would get a share of the profit. Douglas, however, must keep them in repair and check on each service station operator regularly to make sure he's handling his end of the operation. To date, Douglas has fifteen service stations renting bikes and takes in an extra $1500 a month over and above expenses.

This type of operation works well with any kind of small recreational vehicle or boat. You must buy the equipment in the first place, select the areas in which you want to rent, solicit service stations or other small businesses to handle the rentals, and service them regularly.

Service stations probably make the best rental locations for several reasons: there are a tremendous number to choose from, there's room on most service station lots to store and display the vehicles, and most service station operators are on the lookout for almost anything that will bring in added revenue.

Try to select rental locations with a good demand. Bicycles do well almost anywhere there is a place to ride, such as a park. Canoes and boats do well near lakes or rivers. Trailers, campers and tent trailers do well in almost any city location, since they will be pulled (or driven) to recreation areas. Snowmobiles and all-terrain vehicles rent best near where they'll be used.

You'll need a contract for anyone renting your equipment, including an agreement to provide the vehicles at a specified rate (usually the businessman handling the equipment will get from 40 to 50 percent of the total rental fee), the amount he can charge, the deposit he takes, if any, and the type or kind of protection he must provide the vehicles. Here also include provisions for records and upkeep of the vehicles.

You must also provide the businessman handling your vehicles with a standard record sheet that lists whom he has rented to, the number of hours rented and the fees collected.

You will need to establish regular times to collect your

part of the fees and pick up vehicles needing repairs. You should also make spot checks to insure that the rentals are being reported accurately. You can buy new vehicles (including boats) through distributors at less than retail price. Find these by writing to manufacturers. These names are available at the library in the *Thomas Register,* and in such magazines as *Trailer Life,* 23945 Craftsman Rd., Calabasas, Calif. 91302; *Hardware Merchandiser,* 7300 N. Cicero-Lincolnwood, Chicago, Ill. 60646; *American Bicyclist and Motorcyclist,* 461 Eighth Ave., New York, N.Y. 10011. You can also find good used equipment buys by watching the classified section of your local newspaper.

Musical instruments

Music interest today is on the increase, and children everywhere are taking lessons and participating in school bands as they never have before. Most parents, however, want the child to try out an instrument before they invest a large sum of money in it.

This is where your opportunity lies. The demand for musical instrument rentals to this group is booming, and they often keep the rental out for two months to two years.

Best investments are used instruments found through newspaper classified sections ($35 to $200 depending on the instrument). Use the same classified section to advertise your instruments for rent, from $5 to $10 per month.

Back someone else in a spare-time business

People wanting to go into part-time business for themselves often need capital to start. These can be good investments provided you pick carefully. Advertise the fact that you have money available for a part-time business in the classified section of your local newspaper, then screen the prospects carefully. Pick only those that look as if they will make money. Draw up a written agreement (buy these at an office supply store) which includes your participation in the profits, usually 25 to 50 percent.

Using this method Steve Hester, a former $8000 a year janitor who opened a part-time dog grooming service with a $180 income tax refund and parlayed it quickly into a $15,000 a year enterprise, picked out five students at a local college, put up $1000 each, and went into partnership with each in a different kind of part-time business. These included a weekend car wash, a dance band, a day care center for student mothers, a mobile tire service and a college waterbed store. The combined income from these businesses now brings him $60,000 a year, four times his original income, without any extra work on his part.

Vacant land investments

Many cities today ban recreational vehicles (trailers, campers, motor homes) from parking either in driveways or on the streets in residential sections. Owners therefore must rent storage space elsewhere. People owning vacant lots in commercial areas also often welcome interim income while waiting to build or sell. These two factors can provide a good investment opportunity. You can rent or lease the land from the owner and rent out Rec V storage space.

Look up lot owners at the City Hall or the County Courthouse. Most investors try to keep monthly lot rental below $150 and charge Rec V owners from $8 to $15 a month storage (solicited through classified ads).

Many investors also hire a private police protection patrol ($20 to $50 a month) servicing other area merchants, so customers will feel their Rec V's are protected.

Resell used items

Not a typical investment but useful anyway if you're a shrewd buyer and seller. Look in the classified ads to see what a treasure trove is offered there: wheelchairs, space heaters, air compressors, snowmobiles, Rototillers, cribs, reducing machines and a lot more.

One investor constantly scans these sections and buys items he feels are a good value. He then adds on a 30 percent profit for himself and re-advertises in the same classified section.

Although he must handle all sales himself, he often makes a 1000 percent profit on an initial $30 investment over a five or six month period. The trick is to buy the item below actual market value and resell at a profit. Not everyone has this knack, but those who do can make good investment profits.

Need-filling investments

This investment is similar to recreational rental investments, except it utilizes businesses other than service stations, and the item offered fills a need. Good examples of this are TV tube testers, copy machines, card plastic coating machines and similar items. These machines are placed in drug stores, grocery stores, hardware stores and similar retail outlets. You service machines at regular intervals and collect the money. As with recreational rentals, you need a written agreement between you and the store owner which spells out how much he receives, and what his obligations are as well as yours. You can often find these investments listed under *Business Opportunities* in the newspaper classified sections. Some investors are able to make returns up to 20 percent in this area. Often you can start with $500 to $1000 and add to it as you go along.

Equipment rental investments

Very similar to need-filling investments, except the items placed in retail outlets are rented by the store's customers. This includes rug shampooers, floor buffers, exercise equipment, and similar items. Names of manufacturers selling these items can be found in *Rent-all Magazine,* 757 Third Ave., New York, N.Y. 10017.

It's possible to start here with as little as $150. Returns

vary between 15 percent and 70 percent, depending on location, traffic and similar factors. Handle the contract between you and the retail store as you would for similar investments already listed here.

Bulk lot investments

This includes hay, firewood, peat moss, steer manure and many other items. This again is the buy and sell game. Bud Wilson, a $5,900 a year shoe salesman who needed extra cash to support his wife's parents, constantly watches for people felling and trimming trees. He then asks them if they want to sell him the wood. This he cuts into fireplace size and piles high on his front lawn. Backed up with a sign reading *firewood* it usually sells out in a short time. Normally, he figures on making $300 for every $100 he invests. Besides simply looking for home-owners cutting their own trees he also finds his firewood by advertising for it in the classified ads. This adds about $4300 a year to his income, which more than takes care of his wife's parents.

Another small investor, Jerry Keister, a Sacramento, California government clerk, does the same thing with bales of hay. He buys it from local farmers, adds 25¢ a bale, then stacks it on a vacant lot he's rented in a neighborhood where there are many horse owners. To make sales, he puts up a large sign which informs interested buyers that he's only there on Saturday and that they must haul the hay away themselves.

Frequently he sells four or five hundred bales a Saturday this way. His investment for this amount averages $400 to $500, his profit runs from $80 to $125. Not bad for part-time work on Saturdays!

Farm machinery investments

Farmers frequently need extra equipment such as tractors, disc harrows, and similar items. They also have a need for specialized crop handling equipment: rotary cutters, harvesters and more. The more specialized the equipment, the less likely the farmer is to buy it for himself and the more likely you will have a rental market for it.

This equipment can be expensive, however, running from $300 to as high as $17,000–$18,000 and more. Most items run considerably less. You can frequently invest several hundred down and put the rest on payments. Rental fees depend on your investment, but as a rule of thumb figure on making 30 percent a year on every dollar invested.

You can find used equipment by watching the ads under "farm equipment" in the newspaper. You can also find names and addresses of farm equipment manufacturers in *Southern Farm Equipment* magazine, PO Box 6429, Nashville, Tenn. 37122, or *Implement and Tractor* magazine, 1014 Wyandotte St., Kansas City, Mo. 64105.

Resort area re-rentals

Currently cabin rentals in resort areas are booming for both summer and winter use. You can make money on the fact that the weekend or weekly rental rate is far greater than the all-season rate.

Greg Beachum, a San Francisco spare-time businessman and investor, originally was an $8600 a year bus driver but decided he wanted a lot more out of life than that. He sets aside $1000 every winter for ski rental investments. Last winter he rented two A-frame cabins for $500 each for the season, running from the last week in November to the second week in April. He then advertised them under *Mountain Houses—for rent* in the classified section of the paper for $125 a week, $75 a weekend. The results: one cabin brought $1500 for the season, the other approximately $1000, leaving a $1500 profit on his investment. The ads themselves ran continuously at a total of $51.

To find his investment cabins Greg advertises in the classifieds, asking to lease a cabin for the entire winter season. As the offers come in, he selects the area carefully and secures an agreement in writing that states he may rent the cabins or sublease them as he sees fit.

He also hires an older retired couple living near the cabins at $10 a job to clean up after each rental. His work consists of answering the phone and taking reservations. All rentals are payable in advance. Greg's total income for the year now approximates $59,000, out of which he maintains a large home, four cars and a large cabin of his own.

DON'T OVERLOOK CONVENTIONAL INVESTMENTS

Non-conventional investments frequently require less cash to start and sometimes bring higher returns, but you should also consider the possibility of conventional investments for the earnings from your spare-time businesses. These include second mortgages, land, mutual funds, limited partnerships, apartments and duplexes, houses, stocks, investment clubs, and loans. Let's look at each and see how they stand up as an investment.

Second mortgages

Many people today need to borrow money to make the down payment on the home they want, or borrow money on their home for some purpose. You can loan them this $200, $300, $1000 or more, take a second mortgage on their home, get a return up to 18 percent a year and have a protected investment.

If your borrower defaults, you can foreclose the second. The bank or other institution holding the first mortgage must be paid first, but if you are cautious and don't loan more than an amount which together with the first mortgage will be under the market value of the house, your investment will be secure.

You can buy second mortgage agreements at an office supply store. You should also check a potential customer's credit.

Often you can make an arrangement for this through the local Credit Bureau. Sometimes this is in the form of membership or a yearly contract. Your bank can also check credit for you. You can find potential prospects with a small ad under *Real Estate Loans* in your local paper.

Land

You can still make money buying small parcels of land by breaking them into two, three, or four parcels for resale. Start by looking for vacant land for sale in the newspaper classifieds. You must use your own judgment to determine if there's a market for small parcels where you want to buy. Local real estate firms can also advise you of the condition of this market, but don't rely solely on their advice.

Five-acre parcels in this country can be bought for $100 to $15,000 or more depending on the location. A five-acre parcel selling for $1000 can often be divided into four parcels and resold for $500 each.

Financing varies widely. You can sometimes put $50 down on a $1000 parcel and finance the rest at $25 to $50 a month. Typical, however, is $300 down and five to ten year financing at 8 percent to 10 percent interest.

Start by looking at as many parcels in your area as possible, and try to form some idea of the market for small lots. If you must hold for some time before reselling, consider (in figuring possible profits) the taxes, total interest, and payments.

Mutual funds

The advantage of mutual funds is that they have professional money management, they reduce investment risk, and they spread their investment for safety. Funds can be classified by objectives such as growth or income, they can be classified by investments such as specialty funds (chemicals, electronics, aircraft, etc.), or balanced funds which invest in bonds as well as stocks. These funds ordinarily return from 2 percent to 7 percent and up annually.

Some funds have done moderately well, others have fared badly. Best to check their brochures carefully and determine which have performed well. Either the book *Successful Investing Through Mutual Funds* by Robert Frank (Hart Publishing Co., 1969) or *What About Mutual Funds?* by John Straley (Harper and Row, 1967) can give you guidelines for doing this. You can obtain brochures by calling any broker listed in the telephone yellow pages or by answering ads in *The Wall Street Journal*. You can start your investment in some funds with a small amount of money. The books mentioned above will give you the details of how to start your investment and the factors to consider.

Limited partnership syndicates

Limited partnership syndication is simply the pooling of investment dollars by a large number of investors for the acquisition of land, apartments, buildings, or similar income-producing property. The structure consists of a general partner who manages the property and limited partners who share in the profits, but generally have no voice in management. You put in specified amounts, usually from $500 up with monthly payments of between $25 and $50. You can find these limited partnerships advertised in *The Wall Street Journal* or in the financial pages of your local paper.

Apartments and duplexes

More than one millionaire has made his entire fortune in apartment and duplex investments. A great advantage here is that you can start with a small investment ($500 to $3500) and expand as you save the cash. Real estate investment, however, is complicated, and a certain amount of expertise is needed. A good book, such as *How I Turned $100 Into A Million In Real*

Estate—In My Spare Time by William Nickerson (Pocketbooks), *How To Build a Fortune In Real Estate* by Moser (Prentice-Hall), *How To Make Money In Real Estate* by McMichael (Prentice-Hall), or *How Real Estate Fortunes Are Made* by Bockl (Prentice-Hall) will help you through the pitfalls.

Stocks

Stocks can be a good investment area for your spare cash, but again there are many pitfalls. *Proceed cautiously.* A good way to start is to organize an investment club. This consists of your friends, neighbors, or anyone else who is interested in investing. You can put up as little as $50 in the beginning, plus a $15 to $100 a month investment.

After you have the club together, a stock firm (found in the telephone yellow pages) will usually assign a broker to your club. Don't expect to make big money from an investment club, but you can break in this way with little risk. From here you can advance to a larger investment portfolio of your own.

HOW TO MAKE INVESTMENTS FIT YOUR MONEY-MAKING PLANS

After you start to accumulate some surplus cash, investments should always be a part of your money-making plans. The question is, however, how do you make them fit your other activities? The answer is to consider them on a time, labor, dollar, interest, and background basis. If they fit well in most of these areas, then you can probably handle them easily with a minimum of effort. Here are some pointers:

1. *Consider your time involvement:* The more time you spend in work activities, the less you will want to spend managing an investment. For instance, if your part-time activities require 30 hours or more a week, you probably wouldn't want

to spend more than one to ten hours extra in investment activity. On the other hand, if your part-time activities account for only ten hours or so a week, you might welcome a greater time involvement.

A mutual fund investment, for instance, would require almost no time. Recreation spare-time rentals, on the other hand, would require a great deal of personal supervision.

Here are the general time requirements for the investments discussed in this chapter:

> *Large time-consuming investments*—recreational rentals, reselling used items, need filling.
>
> *Medium time-consuming investments*—musical instruments, backing someone else, vacant land, equipment rental, bulk lot, farm machinery, resort area re-rentals, land, apartments and duplexes.
>
> *Little time-consuming investments*—mutual funds, second mortgages, stock. (Stock investments, however, can take large amounts of time, depending on your approach.)

In deciding whether or not an investment fits on a time basis, simply estimate how much time you feel you will need for a particular investment activity, then add it to the time you're already putting in. That will tell you whether or not you can handle that particular investment easily.

2. *Consider the labor needed:* Investments that require a lot of activity go well with part-time enterprises that make few demands, but are bad with spare-time projects that require a great deal of work.

For instance, a 27-year-old Los Angeles factory worker named Bruce Hamilton needed an extra income to bail out a down and out brother. Bruce developed a very successful part-time gourmet food mail order business that brought in almost $18,000 a year. Bruce, however, did part of the processing himself, all of the packaging and mailing, and most of the advertising. This required considerable work.

When he got ready to expand into investments, he started a television tube testing route with an extra $500 that required him to make the rounds of 35 stores twice a week. Within eight weeks Bruce was ready to collapse. He then sold the route at a profit and put his money into mutual funds. Although his return isn't as great, mutual funds fit better with his total activity.

Consider, then, how much actual work each requires and try to match little spare-time work with an active investment, and active spare-time projects with little-time investments.

3. *Consider the money needs:* Whether or not an investment fits your money-making plans also depends on how much money you have to invest, and how much a project takes. Unfortunately, many investors forget this. Greg Randolph, a part-time ski clothing manufacturer grossing almost $30,000 a year, had about $1000 to invest. Unfortunately, he picked a snowmobile rental investment that required $1800 initially, and another $1000 within two months just to keep up with demand. This caused him to take additional money from his part-time business and cut down on supply orders. The result was that overall income dropped until he caught up.

The rule, then, is to invest only extra or surplus money and not draw any capital needed for the business itself. Otherwise the two activities interfere and make each other more difficult.

4. *Consider your own interest:* To be successful with your investments, you must have an overall interest in that type of investment. Henderson Biggot, for instance, a successful part-time printer who ran a $300 investment and 15 hours a week into a $50,000 a year enterprise, couldn't seem to get interested in stocks, yet was convinced by his friends that here is where he should put his money.

As a result, Henderson didn't take enough interest to learn anything about stocks, didn't follow them regularly, or go over his portfolio periodically to weed out the losses.

When his loss at the end of the first year hit $5000, Henderson recognized his mistake, took his money out of the stock market and invested it in duplex rental units. This kind of an investment intrigued him so much he enrolled in a real estate class at a local college, started reading at length about rental investments, and began to look for more duplexes to acquire. At the end of the second year Henderson had recouped his loss and made an additional $2000 profit.

Unfortunately, interest has a great deal to do with just how successful you will be with particular investments. And in order to make investments fit your money-making plans, you must ignore those that hold no interest and consider only those you're willing to work with and learn something about.

5. *Consider your background:* Your background is important in making your investments fit your money-making plans. A background that has something to do with your investment area can often increase your overall investment income considerably.

Dennis Ralston is a San Francisco high school teacher who had played in his grade school, high school and college bands. In addition to teaching, Dennis spent twenty hours a week operating a $25,000 a year part-time advertising service. He had started this business with $100 to pay off some bad debts when his father's business failed. Dennis also found time to compose music and spent considerable time reading about musicians. When he decided to invest $300 in the rental of used musical instruments, he discovered much to his surprise that his background really came in handy.

First, Dennis could talk music and was able to advise parents whether or not he thought their child could be a successful musician and with what instrument. In addition, he was so enthusiastic about music that he often convinced the parents that one of them should take up an instrument at the same time their children did. Also, parents were so impressed with his background and knowledge they sent many friends to him. Within a short time his instruments were booked months in advance, and at the end of the first year his $300 investment had returned well over $3000—enabling him to put a down payment on an airplane he'd been dreaming about for years.

Ron Rouse, on the other hand, a discount store clerk who skyrocketed a $400 investment in a part-time ski cap manufacturing business to an over $150,000 a year gross income, did equally well in the stock market. Ron's father had been interested in stocks all his life and frequently talked over investments with his son. In addition, Ron had spent two years working for the local newspaper as part-time business and financial reporter. During this time he received a thorough grounding in stocks. He read the financial news daily and had a good working knowledge of the language.

When he finally accumulated investment cash, he naturally thought of the stock market. He immediately found he had a natural feel for this type of investment and within a short time bought $600 worth of stock in an automotive hard parts company. Six months later he sold that stock for $1000 profit and invested the entire amount in two recreational vehicle firms. By the end of the the year he had purchased 12 stocks and sold six. Although some did better than others, his overall profit amounted to almost $3000. Ron's background probably didn't account for his entire success, but it certainly helped.

HOW TO TEST YOUR INVESTMENT POSSIBILITIES

There are many kinds of investments. Some will make money, others won't. Investments, however, shouldn't be a guess. Before spending your money you should have some idea of how your investment will do and just what kind of return you can expect.

There are, of course, no accurate formulas, but here are a few guidelines you can follow:

Figure out the possible dollar potential on paper. This is the first step. Naturally it is a guess, but you must start somewhere. Let's take used musical instruments as an example. You find, for instance, that you can buy three cornets and three clarinets (used) for $300. They then rent for $15 a month, $1080 gross a year. Divide your initial investment plus any major expenses for that year in the year's gross. For the musical instruments, this is 360 percent. To find the practical possibilities of this investment, now divide it by three, for 120 percent.

Say, also, that you are considering the possibility of a mutual fund that invests in Government bonds for a 7 percent a year return. Just how do these two stack up? It's impossible to tell at this point. Don't try to make any comparisons. Simply find your possible percentage of gross profit. Next, rate the possible return on this return index. (See Table 11-A.)

Table 11-A

3 to 5%	1
6 to 10%	2
11 to 30%	4
31 to 50%	8
51 to 100%	12
101 to 200%	20
200% and above	30

These figures can be used later to give you an investment index. On this table, the musical instruments rate 20, the mutual fund 2. Go through this procedure for any investments you're considering except stocks. These require a much more complicated analysis. Pick up a book on stocks at any bookstore to help you make your decisions here.

To find the practical net return possibilities, divide musical instrument possible gross for the year by 3 (as done here), recreational rentals 2, backing someone else 4, vacant land improvements 3, reselling used items 3, need-filling investments 3, equipment rental 3, bulk lot investments 2, farm machinery investments 4, resort area re-rentals 4, second mortgages 2, land 2, mutual funds 1, apartments and duplexes 2.

When considering apartments and duplexes, you should be a little more precise than is possible with the above method. Here is a formula that will give you a more accurate dollar potential:

First, estimate your possible yearly rents in dollars. Jot this figure down on a piece of paper, and from it subtract the total cost of your taxes and utilities. This will give you your expected annual income.

If the rent is to be over $200 a month, put down twice the monthly rental. If the building's interior or exterior is in bad shape, deduct 10 percent of the expected annual income. If the yard or grounds around the building are run-down, deduct another 1 percent.

Estimate the value of the location—the building's closeness to schools, stores, etc. If it is in a good location, make no deduction, but if the location is only fair, deduct 5 percent, and if it is poor, deduct 10 percent of the expected annual income. The same is true of the character of the neighborhood—if you rate it "good," make no deduction, but if it is only fair, deduct 5 percent, and if it is poor, deduct 10 percent of the expected annual income.

Add up all the deductions and subtract the figures from the total of the expected annual income, then multiply the remaining figure by seven. This gives you the estimated fair market value.

To get a table value, first find the percentage of income return for your duplex or apartment by dividing your total dollar investment into the total possible return minus the deductions. For example, you put $1000 down on a $20,000 duplex in a fair location in a fair neighborhood. The rent is $150 each side.

The possible yearly income minus taxes here	$3000
Deductions for location and neighborhood	300
	$2700

To get a percentage of gross profit return, divide $1000 into $2700. This gives you 270 percent. Now by following the practice of dividing apartments and duplexes by two to find the practical net percentage return, we get 135 percent. This gives us a figure on the return index (Table 11-A) of 20.

However, this needs adjusting. When we multiply the

$2700 income by 7 to get a fair market value we get $18,900. That's the price we should have paid. But since we overpaid we must subtract from the return index. (See Table 11-B.)

Table 11-B. Amount Paid Over or Under Market Value

$5000 over fair market value	-15
$2000 to $4999 over	-10
$1000 to $1999 over	- 8
$ 500 to $ 999 over	- 6
$ 100 to $ 499 over	- 4
$ 100 to $ 499 under market value	+ 4
$ 500 to $ 999 under	+ 6
$1000 to $1999 under	+ 8
$2000 or more under	+10

Since we paid $1,100 too much, we should subtract 8 points from our 20 to give us *12* on the possible return index table.

We must also treat land separately. Make up a numbered checklist on a sheet of notepaper and rate each factor as "excellent," "good," or "fair."

Table 11-C. Checklist for Successful Land Investment

Population
   1. Present population area
   2. Ten-year population projected growth
Accessibility
   3. Existing freeways
   4. Planned freeways
   5. Airports
   6. Railroads
Employment
   7. Industry
   8. Construction
   9. Tourist
   10. Commercial Business
Water
   11. Existing
   12. Planned

Climate
   13. Average summer
   14. Summer high
   15. Winter low
   16. Amount of rainfall
Topography
   17. Level, compared to sea-level
   18. Grade of hills
Recreation
   19. Hunting
   20. Fishing
   21. Boating
   22. Skiing
   23. Ocean
   24. Golf
Metropolitan area
   25. Distance
      (Within 0–50 miles is excellent, 50–100 miles is good, 100–150 miles is fair)
   26. Population size
      (Over 100,000 is excellent, 25,000 to 100,000 is good, under 25,000 is fair)

To use this chart effectively, find the possible percentage return on your land investment per year. Check with local real estate offices to find about how much raw land has been increasing per year in your area, then figure the percentage increase on your investment. For instance, if land in your part of the city has been increasing 10 percent in value every year and you can buy an acre for $1000 with $200 down, you can reasonably expect your lot to be worth $1100 in a year—which means you received $100 for your $200 investment, or a 50 percent increase. To find practical return possibilities, divide by 1 to give you 50 percent.

Now, however, you must deduct from the checklist for successful land investment. Grade each category: population, accessibility, etc. Subtract one percentage point for every two "good" ratings, and one point for each "fair" rating. Next look up the return index in Table 11-A.

Make a sample investment. Sometimes you will actually make a trial investment, other times you can dry run. You can, for instance, buy one musical instrument and try renting it. The investment is small, but you don't want to invest $1800 in a trailer just to see how it will go. You can, however, do it by "proxy." Many small rental yards keep one or two trailers for rental. Spot one, and over a three-month period keep track of how many times that particular trailer is out. This will take work, but it may well mean money in your pocket in the long run.

In the meantime, call the rental yard for their rates. Look up the address of that particular trailer manufacturer in the *Thomas Register* (found in the Library Reference Room). Write him for the wholesale price for rental purposes or ask to be referred to a distributor who can give you a price. Once you have a cost figure and know how much a particular yard made in a three-month period, you can figure out possible yearly income and a possible percentage of return. Compensate for the time of year you took your sample. Summer rentals are best, spring and fall only fair, winter poor. Now let's take an example:

Say you discover you can buy a trailer at $1200 with $200 down and $50 a month (through a bank loan). You also discover that one firm renting these trailers has them out about 20 weeks a year at $50 a week ($1000). Subtract your total payment of $600 for the first year from your probable return and you have $400 left. On an initial investment of $200 this gives you a 100 percent return. Going by our rule again, however, divide it by two for 50 percent and look up the return index in Table 11-A. It comes out to 8.

To figure the returns on other types of investments you will need some imagination, but basically you must spot someone doing something similar and observe him as closely as possible over a several-month period.

Get outside opinions. If possible, go to an outsider who knows something about what you want to do and who will give you an opinion. If you're considering an investment in television tube testers, for instance, go to a small business owner who has one in the store and ask him for an opinion. For resort re-rental, call cabin owners listed in the paper and ask what they think. For second mortgage investments, try to find someone with experience and ask his opinion. These people don't have to be experts, but should have some knowledge about these particular investment areas. Now rate them as to what they think: good, fair, poor. Assign ten points for good, five for fair, nothing for poor.

Go to the experts. Try to find someone who really knows something about your investment area. With recreational rentals, for instance, go directly to a rental operator and ask his opinion. Consider these opinions only as a part of your evaluation, however. Since many times "experts" have their own interests at heart or fail to see the overall picture of what you're trying to do, their opinions have only limited value. To get opinions on real estate or second mortgages, go to your local banker. For stocks and mutual funds, go to a local brokerage firm. Here are some other possibilities: musical instruments, a local music store renting instruments; backing someone else, your local banker; vacant land, a real estate broker; used items, a second-hand store; need filling, go to firms who are in the business; rental equipment, rental equipment firms; bulk lot investments, talk to people advertising this item in the newspaper classifieds; farm machinery, go to a rental firm specializing in farm equipment.

As before, rate these opinions good, fair, and poor—assign ten points for good, five for fair, and nothing for poor.

Look within yourself. Finally, ask yourself how you really feel about this investment and give it as honest a rating as you can, again grading good, fair, and poor—assigning ten points for good, five for fair, and nothing for poor. Don't try to do this, however, until you have completed all other ratings. After you have worked with this investment awhile you will begin to understand just how good it is. Unless you have spent time doing the other ratings honestly and in complete detail, however, you simply will not have accumulated the experience necessary for an accurate opinion.

Now you are ready to make an evaluation. Add all the points together. This includes the return index number from figuring out the dollar percentage potential and the sample investment, plus the ratings of knowledgeable people, experts, and yourself. Now divide by the total number of items used for your evaluation. You may leave out one evaluation item if you like.

Before making your final evaluation, consider one other factor—the stability of the investment. A savings account, for instance, is extremely stable; gambling is unstable. When you have completed your initial calculations (obtained by adding all the points together from the dollar percentage potential, the sample investment, knowledgeable people, experts, and your own opinion), then add a stability factor to this, obtained from the Stability Table (Table 11-D).

Table 11-D. Stability Table

Recreational rentals	3
Musical instruments	2
Backing someone else	0
Vacant land improvements	4
Reselling used items	3
Need-filling investments	3
Equipment rental	3
Bulk lot investments	2
Farm machinery investments	2
Resort area re-rentals	0
Second mortgages	5
Land	8
Mutual funds	10
Apartments and duplexes	10

Now evaluate your investment chances—the sum of the investment possibilities and the stability factor from Table 11-D— on the Investment Success Table (Table 11-E).

Table 11-E. Investment Success Table

0 to 5	bad
6 to 9	poor
10 to 15	fair
16 to 20	good
21 to 30	very good
30 and above	excellent

Let's look at a few examples:

You decide to go into resort re-rentals in California and find you can rent a cabin on a yearly basis for $200 a month. You estimate you can re-rent it reasonably, 35 weeks out of the year at $180 a week. This figure is obtained by surveying nearby cabin owners. Total investment, then, is $2400, your total possible income $6300, or 262 percent on investment. To find the possible net return possibilities, divide by four (as noted earlier in this chapter). This gives 65 percent. Then look up the investment index in Table 11-A, giving an investment index of 12. Since taking a sample is extremely hard in this case, eliminate that step. Other cabin owners say that this investment is just fair because of having to clean up after each rental (5 points), local real estate people say the investment is only fair (5 points), and you evaluate it as fair (5 points). Now add it all together:

Dollar potential investment index	12
Knowledgeable people's opinion	5
Expert's opinion	5
Your opinion	5
Total	27
Divide by 4 - approx.	7
Add the stability factor from Table 11-D	0
Total	7

Now look up the success possibility or investment rating in Table 11-E. This investment then rates poor.

Compare this to a mutual fund yielding 7 percent per year. This gives a return index of 2 from Table 11-A, other investors rate this as good (10 points), experts rate it as good (10 points), and you rate it as good (10 points).

Dollar potential investment index	2
Knowledgeable people's opinion	10
Expert's opinion	10
Your opinion	10
Total	32

Divide by 4 =	8
Add the stability factor from Table 11-D =	10
Total	18

Table 11-E then indicates the investment is good.

HOW TO GET THE MOST OUT OF EVERY INVESTMENT

Making your investment pay off means managing your investments efficiently. This involves keeping your dollars working at all times, keeping good investment records, shifting your money from unprofitable investment areas, reviewing investments regularly, soliciting referrals, being alert to the possibilities of selling at a profit, and having an investment plan. Look at each separately.

Keep your dollars working

Unless you keep constant watch, it's possible for some of your investment dollars to stop working. Brighton Reynolds, for instance, a Denver government worker who parlayed a $300 nest egg into a $35,000 a year book mail-order business, decided to invest in bicycle rentals at a number of local service stations. Brighton, however, had his money invested a full six months before he discovered that one station locked the bikes up during the week and refused to rent any day but Saturday. This in effect tied up his working dollars for six days a week. He then moved the bikes to another service station and immediately upped his overall return by 5 percent.

This rule applies to every kind of investment. If, for instance, a homeowner stops paying on a second mortgage, he in effect has tied up your working dollars. If you do not bring this mortgage current immediately, you have lost the use of that money for re-investment purposes, plus any collection costs you may have.

To keep your money working, then, you must review constantly and stay on the alert for problem areas.

Keep good investment records

Records in investing are as important as any other business record. You must always know where your money is and just how much it's making.

When Brighton Reynolds started his bicycle investment, he put ten bikes out to each station. Shortly afterwards, however, several stations asked for more, a few wanted some bikes removed, and others wanted some bikes taken back and others brought out. Since Brighton did not keep exact inventory records of where his bikes were and did not record each transaction, he soon lost track of just who had how many bikes. As a result, when his overall count showed five bikes missing he had no way of knowing which station was responsible. He simply had to assume the loss himself and vow to keep better records in the future.

You should, then, keep records showing how much you've invested, exactly what you've invested in, how many units you have, what the costs are, and where each piece of equipment or investment unit is, plus anything else needed to help keep track of your money.

Shift money from unprofitable investment areas

At the end of the first year in the bicycle rental business, Brighton Reynolds decided to add a few All-Terrain Vehicles at some outlying areas. Within four months, however, Brighton found the ATV's weren't renting and that each was losing money.

Instead of trying to keep these vehicles going, he immediately advertised and sold them at a $300 loss, putting the remaining money back into bicycles. While Brighton did take a loss, at lease he got his money working profitably again. This is what you must do. Review each area every month and get rid of those areas that aren't making money and look as if they won't for a long period of time.

Review investments regularly

Unfortunately it's impossible at any time to invest money and forget it. You must constantly keep on top of what's going on. At the end of the first year with Brighton Reynold's bicycle investment, for instance, bicycle rentals dropped off in several areas. Brighton, however, was concerned with other things. He had turned the servicing and collection over to someone else several months before and didn't realize what was happening. As a result he did nothing. When Brighton finally woke up to what was going on, bicycle rentals at three stations were losing money and just breaking even at one other. This principle of reviewing investments regularly applies to all investment areas. Conditions can change, and you'd better be aware before it costs you money.

Solicit referrals

Not all investments lend themselves to referrals, but many do. People you hold second mortgages for can send friends for this kind of financing, bicycle rental customers can refer others, people who use photocopy services can talk about it, and so forth. The rule is, simply ask people you come in contact with to refer others. For less personal investment areas you can use brochures or printed solicitation.

Sell when you can make a good profit

After two years of bicycle rentals, Brighton received an offer from a firm to buy his complete bicycle investment for $25,000. This was several times the $3000 he had put in. Therefore he sold, took the money, put $3000 into a similar investment enterprise in a neighboring city and invested the rest in stocks and mutual funds. Selling is, in effect, pyramiding. You can then take this money, start again somewhere else, and still have money left for additional investing. The rule is, however, don't sell until you can at least double the total amount you've put in.

Have an investment plan

Always have a general idea of where you want to go. If you've decided to invest in bicycle rentals, for instance, you might lay out a plan that says you'll establish 15 rental stations in your city, then spread to three neighboring communities. After this you'll add motorcycles, snowmobiles, and small trailers to your rental line.

This kind of planning lets you know about where you're going next, avoids duplication, and in some cases allows you to save money by making similar expenditures only once instead of three or four times. All plans, however, should be flexible, since you want to be able to keep your money growing and withdraw from any area that looks like a loser.

HOW TO PYRAMID EVERY INVESTMENT

Investments themselves will, of course, make money. But you can make even more by using pyramiding techniques that will double and triple effective multiplying power of your investments. Here are some techniques you can use:

Put profits back in

Investment profits working for you can produce that much more income. Ray Mendals, a San Francisco utility worker, parlayed a $200 investment into a $100,000 a year part-time candle business. He then invested $1000 in an older duplex, and saved all profits until he had an additional $1000, and bought another duplex. Within three years Ray had 15 duplexes, and a gross investment income of $4000 a month. Investment profits re-invested simply help you reach your money goals that much faster.

Sell and buy regularly

Once you start investing, you'll find that there is a regular buy and sell cycle that will enable you to make additional money. Good activity always makes your investment go up. Ray Mendals learned this early in the game. He bought an older duplex for $15,000, invested another $200 in paint, then rented it for $130 each side. He then put an ad in the local paper advertising it for sale at $18,000. Within three hours after the paper came out, he sold it at full price. With the profit, he simply turned around and bought three more duplexes. Practically every investment has a time when it's worth more than you initially invested. Try to become aware of this increase and offer your investment for sale at that time, provided you can at least double the amount of money you put in.

Use leverage whenever possible

Leverage simply means controlling as much money as possible with a minimum of your own cash. Say you buy $10,000 worth of land for 10 percent down ($1000) and it increased 50 percent in value within three years. You then sell this land, take your $5000 plus equity, and invest in land worth $50,000. You in effect control $50,000 with only $1000 of your own money (plus payments). Try to do this with every investment you make. Keep your original investment and payments as low as possible while acquiring as much cash value as possible.

Use the pyramid method

Good pyramiding requires both leverage and an increase in value of your investment. This method is often used to good advantage with land, but it can be applied to other investments also.

Let's say you buy an acre parcel for $2000 with 10 percent down and it increases 50 percent in three years. You then take your $1000 plus equity and buy a 12-acre parcel for $10,000 (with $1000 down). This is leverage. You then subdivide your parcel into 12 one-acre lots and sell them for $2000 each, or $24,000, leaving you with approximately $14,000. You then take half of this, buy 50 acres and start subdividing all over again. Using this method, some sharp land investors over the last ten years have managed to run an original $1000 into well over a million.

The secret here is to divide your investment into smaller pieces, selling at a larger amount per unit than you could get for these same units when sold as a larger piece. Pyramiding works well in many investment areas and can increase profits spectacularly.

Try to make one investment lead to others

One investment should actually trigger another. Once you start investing in duplexes, for instance, you almost automatically start looking for the next, and if you let it be known you're in the market they'll come to you.

This is true in most other areas. Bicycle rentals, for instance, lead almost automatically to motorcycles, ATV's and other recreational rentals. And once you let the word out that you're open to other locations and items, they'll automatically start coming to you. Simply talk about it to anyone who seems interested.

KEEP THESE INVESTMENT FACTORS IN MIND

Investments, like all other aspects of business, follow certain rules Here are several you should keep in mind as you start your investment activity:

Don't invest until you have extra money: Investment money should be extra money. Money taken from your business that will hamper or slow it down creates a further problem.

Consider your investment expenses: Investment expenses must be kept low if you expect to make money. Avoid any investments which require monthly expenditures in excess of 3 percent of your original investment (payments on the investment itself excepted).

Make sure that borrowed money makes money: Borrowed money has one purpose, to make more money. Do not borrow money for living expenses, office extras or frills. Borrow only when you intend to re-invest for greater profits.

Watch the economy closely: Some investments bring better returns at some times than at others. When the economy slows down, for instance, some recreational activities also slow down. In addition, second mortgages return more on the investment when money is harder to get. The need for apartments and duplexes also goes up and down depending on local conditions. Watch closely how your particular investment behaves and react accordingly.

Make sure your investment produces a better percentage return than that same money would make invested in your spare-time business. If your investment money produces just as well in your business, then you might as well keep it there in the first place. Investments must produce a greater return to be worthwhile. Check this closely before investing.